Avidly Reads

Avidly Reads

General Editors: Sarah Mesle and Sarah Blackwood

The Avidly Reads series presents brief books about how culture makes us feel. We invite readers and writers to indulge feelings—and to tell their stories—in the idiom that distinguishes the best conversations about culture.

Avidly Reads: Theory
Jordan Alexander Stein

Avidly Reads: Board Games
Eric Thurm

Avidly Reads: Making Out
Kathryn Bond Stockton

Avidly Reads: Passages
Michelle D. Commander

Avidly Reads: Guilty Pleasures
Arielle Zibrak

Guilty Pleasures

ARIELLE ZIBRAK

NEW YORK UNIVERSITY PRESS *New York*

NEW YORK UNIVERSITY PRESS
New York
www.nyupress.org

© 2021 by New York University
All rights reserved

References to Internet websites (URLs) were accurate at the time of writing. Neither the author nor New York University Press is responsible for URLs that may have expired or changed since the manuscript was prepared.

Cataloging-in-Publication data is available from the publisher.
ISBN 9781479807079 (hardcover)
ISBN 9781479807093 (paperback)
ISBN 9781479807109 (consumer ebook)
ISBN 9781479807123 (library ebook)

New York University Press books are printed on acid-free paper, and their binding materials are chosen for strength and durability. We strive to use environmentally responsible suppliers and materials to the greatest extent possible in publishing our books.

Manufactured in the United States of America

10 9 8 7 6 5 4 3 2 1

Also available as an ebook

For H., for making a strong case for love

Contents

INTRODUCTION

Anyone who's worth anything reads just what
he likes, as the mood takes him, and with ex-
travagant enthusiasm.
—Virginia Woolf

The one way of not doing anything about a
situation is feeling guilty about it.
—Alan Watts

Because I didn't learn to read in school, I never
learned which books were worth reading. Both of
my parents were the first in their families to graduate from college. My mother majored in English, my
father in philosophy. The walls in our little 1920s
Tudor were lined with their hard-won college books.
My mom's loopy adolescent handwriting, which she
retained into adulthood, boldly speculated about the
characters in the margins; my dad's more restrained
scratchings noted references and defined terms. My
parents and I didn't read together much past early
childhood, but they spoke to me about books well
into my adolescence through this cryptic marginalia.
Sitting with their worn paperbacks, I felt closer to

some version of them that I was otherwise convinced I'd missed out on entirely; the love I longed to receive from them seemed visible, right there, expressed in the negative space of the pages. In this way, I learned early on that reading, even and maybe especially promiscuous reading, offers us love as an available pleasure. That insight shapes what's to come, in this book about the mixed emotions of our unruly media encounters.

By the time I was in junior high, I'd read almost every book in the house. This included, most memorably, *Fear and Trembling*, *Lolita*, Shakespeare's comedies and tragedies (but not histories—my mom must not have taken that course), *Thus Spake Zarathustra*, *Nausea*, *The Brothers Karamazov*, *David Copperfield*—works I enjoyed in part because most of them flew completely over my head. Reading them was like talking with someone much older and smarter who is also very good-looking. I chose *Lolita* as a subject for the fifth-grade book presentation I delivered in homeroom, somehow missing the sexual relationship in that novel altogether. At the time, I understood it as the story of an overprotective stepfather who takes his daughter on a very interesting vacation. My middle-aged, male homeroom teacher corrected me only on the pronunciation of the author's name.

There were other books on those shelves I recall reading with equal fascination—*The Joy of Sex*, a biography of Michael Jackson (with full color photographs!), *The Valley of the Dolls*, *Pet Sematary*, *The Bell Jar*, and my most beloved *If Life Is a Bowl of Cherries, What Am I Doing in the Pits?* by Erma Bombeck. I was also hanging out at the library a lot. There was a version of myself I could be there, in the bookstacks, that I couldn't be anywhere else—or maybe it's that I was thinking about the grown female person I would someday become. I'd ride my bike to the local public library after school and wander the shelves, pulling out whatever volume had the most intriguing title, sitting down on the floor to read most of it there, and only occasionally taking books out. For some reason, I had and still have a lot of anxiety about losing or ruining library books and so have always preferred to own my own copies whenever possible. I think this is due, in part, to my fondness for reading while eating soup (my personal library also serves as a history of various soups consumed). But no matter, because the public library of my childhood hometown became off-limits to me in junior high after reports circulated of a pedophile lurking there and flashing young girls through the shelves. This is true: if you want to see it as a metaphor for the way girlish reading is haunted by the specter of dangerous desire, well, that's maybe another part of where this story is going.

Anyway, then my mom started taking me to what will forever remain my cathedral: a magical discount bookstore called the New England Mobile Book Fair. This store began as a van full of used books—hence the "mobile"—but by my formative years, it had expanded to a massive, high-ceilinged warehouse blindingly illuminated by fluorescent bulbs, where books were arranged neither by genre nor by author but by publisher and, within publisher, by ISBN. This method of stocking the books had a profound impact on my life.

Like the books in my house, which were arranged in no particular order whatsoever, the New England Mobile Book Fair suffered no generic predeterminations or qualifiers. "Literary fiction," "romance," "mystery," "nonfiction," "self-help," "humor"—they were all more or less mixed together. Each volume had its own bits of wisdom to impart, its little jokes. They all equally allowed me to be alone in the presence of others. I loved them indiscriminately. I read from all of the genres listed above but did tend to gravitate more toward novels. My mother adopted the same rule for the bookstore that my father had pioneered for the candy store: I could pick five things. Just as at the candy story I had learned to select bagged gummies and Big League Chew over less generous offerings, regardless of flavor, at the bookstore I combed the shelves for the thickest works.

I learned to love novels that went on and on, mass-market paperbacks with text blocks thick enough for doodling on the soft edges, clunky tomes that ended up clocking a lot of hours in my backpack, their signatures falling out in chunks as the spinal glue dried and flaked off. Besides their virtues of economy, long novels were also a salve to the dread I routinely experienced upon realizing I was near done with a novel that was not a part of a series. It was only much later in my life that I discovered the pleasures of rereading; therefore, at this early point, the ending of a book meant to me the death of all it contained, a thought so unbearable that it nearly soured me on the whole experience altogether. But long novels postponed that dread, and having to experience it less frequently, even if more acutely for having known their characters so well, seemed to make it more bearable.

I think it was mostly by this selection process that I grew up to become a professor of nineteenth-century novels, which tend to be quite long. At the time, I didn't think too much about how most of my reading was set in the same period, a hundred or more years before my own life. I just knew it was set in another place. That, too, was a part of its appeal. (I think for a few years I might have harbored a vague idea, however, especially as regards the fiction of Charles Dickens and L. M. Montgomery, that England and its cousin Canada were curiously devoid of modern conveniences.)

What I'm describing here was my reading experience straight up until college. I was a halfhearted and inconsistent attender of high school, though an avid reader throughout. By this time, I was cutting class and taking public transportation to the Boston Public Library, where I read compulsively and with a similar disregard for what I was reading, still favoring the serial and the long. When my high school English assignment regarded a book I'd already read, I'd complete it. When it didn't, I most often would not. Something within me deeply resented being told what to read. I may have appeared to be nearly failing out of school, but I was actually waiting patiently to be assigned an essay on *If Life Is a Bowl of Cherries, What Am I Doing in the Pits?*, which I would have written with rapturous abandon. Alas, that day never came.

In some ways, this book is that essay. It's not about *If Life Is a Bowl of Cherries, What Am I Doing in the Pits?* (sorry to disappoint any Bombeck-heads out there), but it is about belatedly encountering, and then recovering from, the idea that some books are worth reading and others are not, that some films are shameful to watch, whereas others should be casually mentioned as favorites every chance you get. When social media memes like "the twenty films that changed my life" roll around, I basically want to crawl into a cave and watch Hallmark movies on my iPad until the flood claims us all because I get that *The 39 Steps* is a remarkable artistic achievement, but where is *Overboard*, my friends? Where is *Waiting to Exhale* and *Practical Magic* and *Pretty Woman*? Smart people consume these films, too, and they have as much to tell us about ourselves and the world as the books I picked because I liked their covers or their length or because, like many of the things and people I love most in the world, they just happened to be where I was.

There's a term for this shameful relation to the media that selects us simply by being there when we're not busy doing something more intentional or praiseworthy. That term is the title of this book.

* * *

When someone refers to a guilty pleasure, they're usually making a kind of narcissistic claim about a textual object that is attractive to yet beneath them: "I mostly read the *New Yorker*, but *US Weekly* is my guilty pleasure." I think a more accurate term for the "guilt" implied in this kind of statement may be "shame." When someone says something like this, they seem to mean they're ashamed because they know how bad it is but enjoy it nonetheless in spite of that shame.

The author and speaker Brené Brown, a self-defined "shame researcher," writes that there is "a profound difference" between shame and guilt, primarily because she sees guilt as productive—a place where we can identify how to improve our lives by aligning our actions with our values—whereas shame is an unproductive welter of negative feelings.

My sense of shame is different from Brown's. I'm less interested in what we do with those feelings than I am in why we have them. I'm also a little skeptical of any emotional logic that holds productivity as a guiding virtue. A fundamental proposition of this book is that not everything in our lives has to be "productive" in the forward-looking sense or aligned with our values or even the kind of "positivity" defined by motivational posters with images of icebergs or sunsets or small animals in compromised circumstances. I think the pervasive demand that people—especially female people—be productive and positive produces the majority of the guilt and shame we experience. I can't condone advice to smile more or work harder. The only general advice I can get behind is along the lines of "travel abroad" or "take a bath"—means to no clear end or product beyond themselves. Travel because other places have better food and different languages. Take a bath because the point of a bath is the bath. I find that enormously edifying. With Kant, I urge us to act as if our bath pleasure is not a means to an end but rather an end in itself.

Guilty pleasure texts are like baths for the mind. They're usually cast as mindless or unproductive. My first objection here is, predictably, that therein lies a particularly bad account of productivity. Pleasure is productive; it produces itself. My second is that if you're a thinking person, you can think "productively" through any object—an essay by Susan Sontag or a Ke$ha lyric—and if NPR ever asked for my "This I Believe" statement, I would say, with Virginia Woolf, that I think people should consume whatever media they like without any sense of shame or pride. While I'm at it, I'd also like to ask why the guys I internet-dated in the aughts lied about having read all of the Faulkner or Joyce novels they claimed to have read on their profiles. It's a curious, and frankly puritanical, notion that what you consume defines you or—worse—ranks you, that a person is only as good or as terrible as their most-listened-to songs and the spines on their shelves.

My mentioning here of internet-dating is not merely casual, because once again it demonstrates how reading attaches to our sense of the love we deserve. Those dudes advertised Faulkner, I guess, because they were trying to position themselves as worthy of a Faulkner-quality love—sophisticated, serious, complex? This is a disturbing thought in several respects, and yet it also raises the fascinating question of why and how Faulkner-love raises itself above, say, a *Baby-Sitters Club* kind of love. To answer this question, some literary criticism may be helpful.

I was born at the end of 1981, the same year that the literary scholar Fredric Jameson published his landmark work *The Political Unconscious*, a book that has shaped my thinking in so many ways that I'm continually disappointed that I didn't write it myself before I was born. In it, he argues that history itself is a narrative that unfolds alongside the other narratives—for instance, fictions—that shape our culture. According to Jameson, we can't separate the two by attempting to interpret fictions outside of their political or historical context, nor can we understand our own history without understanding our fictions. Jameson's interpretive project develops out of his cultural understanding: we tend to think of the unconscious as an individually experienced phenomenon. But cultures, he claims, have unconsciousnesses, too. Documents of popular culture, in particular, tell us a lot about what the people who created and consumed them were thinking, feeling, and desiring. If ship manifests and medical records and military logs and patent files are the kinds of documents that reveal the history of our migrations, conflicts, and technologies, popular fictions are the kinds of documents that tell us about the history of our hearts and minds.

A sadly unsurprising thing about *The Political Unconscious* is that Jameson makes his argument through interpreting fiction written almost exclusively by white men.* (Obviously, prebirth me would have done otherwise.) The very white maleness of his work is one reason why scholars, myself included, have long perceived it as Extremely Important. In a review of Emily Nussbaum's *I Like to Watch*, the critic Sarah Mesle identifies the source of this phenomenon as the "circular logic by which a piece of art becomes serious because a serious critic attends to it, and a critic becomes serious by tending to serious art." The prevalence of this brand of logic also explains why the history of men, like the fiction and culture of men, is almost always taken to be more *serious* than the history of women.

My point in raising Jameson—in veering precipitously toward Serious Pleasure rather than the

---

* Jameson doesn't actually mention Faulkner but does mention Joyce.

guilty kind you came here to read about—is that I want to take Jameson both as a useful thinker *and* as an example of the unconscious he's describing: *The Political Unconscious* is a document of an intellectual unconscious whereby male things are the ones that tell us what "our" collective unconscious is like. This book you are reading, on the other hand, is not very interested in that. Guilty pleasures, I am going to propose, reveal a collective unconscious of a consciousness that Jameson ignored: the femme one.

When I was taught history in high school, it was the ~~serious~~ male kind. My class was held in a room encircled by a wallpaper border depicting the presidents of the United States of America (unfortunately, not the nineties alt-rock band that recorded "Peaches" but the actual leaders of the nation in which I was born). So, like many of you I'm sure, I was forced to sit in a space that was literally covered in the faces of white men while a white man told me to read about and memorize the names of white men and the things they did. I understand why white men like this history; it belongs to them. But I have heard enough of it and no longer find it very interesting. To me, learning this history over and over again is like having a conversation with someone who only talks about himself. No matter how many things he's done or how witty or insightful his ideas may be, at a certain point you're going to need to switch topics or say you have to use the restroom and politely walk away forever.

When I teach American literature, I tend to focus on work by women writers, queer writers, and writers of color for no better reason than that I find these works more interesting to read. Most of my students do, too, but sometimes I get a complaint. "Why don't we learn more about war?" some students have asked. "We do learn about war," I reply, citing Richard Wright's 1940 *Native Son*, which is about systemic racism, midcentury communist sympathy and its vilification, and widespread physical violence. Those are wars. Students tell me these are not the wars they mean. I tell them how Edith Wharton's 1920 *The Age of Innocence* is about the aftermath of World War I—a good, solid white man's war. They shake their heads. But then, sometimes, they come to see how it is true. It was only when I got to college myself that I really understood that history could be something other than leaders and battles and captains of industry. I took a course called Women in Europe that was a history of the lives of women—a revelation! I immediately became a history major.

Of course, the women who've written novels throughout history do the exact same thing that Jameson's male novelists do. They narrate the psychic and emotional history of another time—*their* psychic and emotional history. Louisa May Alcott's 1869 *Little Women*, for example, is also a novel about a war—the American Civil War—but unlike Stephen Crane's snooze of a novel *The Red Badge of Courage* (1895), it's not about the men on the battlefield. It's about the women at home, who are doing real, serious, important things as well. These women may be more left out of History, but they were not left out of life; and what happened off the battlefield is just as important as what happened on it. Despite this and even how beloved and respected Alcott's novel is, I don't often see people carrying around a prestige copy of *Little Women* the way they might *Moby Dick* or *Ulysses* or *Gravity's Rainbow* or *Infinite Jest*. But *Little Women* and other novels written by the women of the past can also make you smarter if you actually read them. And they have a lot to tell us about what people were like then and how we became who we are now. This is why many of us find reading these books so deeply pleasurable, even as we may feel ashamed of that pleasure, because so much of our world has told us that this kind of becoming isn't important, that it (and we) don't matter.

In addition to revealing some truths about our collective unconscious, novels help us to work through whatever it is we're dealing with as a society and as individuals. If anything about this kind of media consumption is self-definitional, it's the shame associated with it—not because "guilty pleasures" reveal some fundamental truths about the consumer's lowbrow aesthetic tendencies but because a lot of the genres of movies and television that get referred to as "guilty pleasures" are also another kind of guilty pleasure, what I like to think of as the Hester Prynne kind, where guilt *is* what's being pleasurably stimulated alongside libidos and baser desires for nice hair and fancy things.

In this sense, I can accept the category of "guilty pleasures" as a name for things that give us this pleasurable release from guilt and shame or space to dwell within it. And, in general, I think many Americans of many different gender circumstances prefer their pleasures guilty. This is a country that advertises potato chips with the slogan "bet you can't have just one," where *Titanic* and *Jurassic Park* (two of the highest grossing films of all time) both have the same general plot: some novel delights immediately followed by sudden mass death. One easy answer is to blame the Puritans—Nathaniel Hawthorne did. His 1850 novel *The Scarlet Letter* is basically the textbook on guilty pleasure.

In my memory, my classmates and I were assigned this book more than once in high school and maybe another couple of times before that in junior high. (I'd already read my mother's college copy early on, selected for priority status because it had a monochromatic print of a lady in a bonnet on it.) Because I grew up in Massachusetts, when we weren't reading *The Scarlet Letter*, we were on seemingly constant field trips to Salem to learn about the witch trials for the fourth or fifth time; then we'd swing by the House of the Seven Gables and the Custom House where Hawthorne worked and learn about Hawthorne and *The Scarlet Letter* all over again for good measure.* I claimed in my tenth-grade paper on this one book that every single American teenager seems to be made to read that Hester Prynne, the infamous adulteress forced into wearing the letter *A*, *likes* her punishment. I based this claim primarily on this passage: "On the breast of her gown, in fine red cloth, surrounded with an elaborate embroidery and fantastic flourishes of gold-thread, appeared the letter *A*. It was so artistically done, and with so much fertility and gorgeous luxuriance of fancy, that it had all the effect of a last and fitting decoration to the apparel which she wore." This was my favorite part of the book. First, it was undeniably punk that she went in this over-the-top direction with a sartorial mandate. Second, the language here about a patch sewn onto a puritan dress for punishment is somehow just oozing with sensual pleasure: fantastic flourishes, gorgeous luxuriance of fancy, *fertility*. I submitted a paper explaining this in slightly different words to my teacher, who did not like the argument. She sat me down, sitcom-style, to explain that this was a text about ostracism and group think and for me to suggest that Hester Prynne took pleasure—let alone sensual pleasure—in her guilt and punishment was very disturbing and wrong-headed.

I can't bear a grudge against this teacher because I respect anyone who teaches high school English (I

---

* We'd go to Thoreau's cabin site at Walden, too, but never the Alcott house or the Dickinson house, which were certainly within easy bus distance.

didn't then, so this blind respect is my best consolation) and also because our field-trip pattern had *The Scarlet Letter* so thoroughly mixed up with the real historical witch trials in everyone's minds, but I did feel a surge of triumph when I later encountered the fact that my paper wasn't very far off from one of the most prevalent critical readings of the novel since 1960, when the literary critic Leslie Fiedler argued that *The Scarlet Letter* is definitely about the fraught nature of sexual desire in America. Fiedler claimed that American literature is incapable of depicting mature sexual relationships—that it falls back on the eroticization of children, unconsummated sexual love between men, and "old maids." (He was smart but totally a man of his time.) For Fiedler, *The Scarlet Letter* was the sexiest book in the canon of great American literature, though, tellingly, all of the sex happens before the book even begins—like if *Crime and Punishment* were just the brutally boring punishment part. While Fiedler emphasized sexual desire as the fulcrum of the novel, he also acknowledged— like most of the novel's readers before him—that its central theme is undeniably guilt, asking why, to Hawthorne (not just the Puritans), "is gorgeousness a trap and love a crime, why beauty forbidden and joy banned?" To which I'd answer: because for a lot of people these things, freely given, would be less pleasurable. It's not as if the pleasure is one thing and the guilt is another. Perhaps guilt kills Dimmesdale, but Hester thrives on it. And so do readers along with her. *The Scarlet Letter* shows us that the pleasures of the sex you can't have or see are inextricable from the guilt that is yours for the taking.

If you watch the 1995 film version of *The Scarlet Letter*, starring Demi Moore, you'll see that the filmmakers get the sexiness part right but miss both most of the guilt and how important it is that no sex happens in the novel. In the novel, the readers only get the pleasure of the implied sex through the author's refusal to give it to us. If we saw Hester and Dimmesdale getting it on, it would be a bad book in 1850 to say the least. When we see it in 1995, it's still a bad movie—especially since the sex scenes are bizarrely interspersed with some impressionistic montage sequences. It's not a very good adaptation of the main themes of Hawthorne's novel if it's full of Demi Moore taking long baths and having her farthingale slowly unlaced by Gary Oldman. But neither can you take *all* of the sex out of *The Scarlet Letter*, implications included.

The updated-for-our-times 2010 version starring Emma Stone, *Easy A*, gets the guilt part right but is pretty rigorously unsexy. The center of the plot is actually the revised fact that the Hester character is a virgin. She fabricates the story of her tryst, so we don't even get to imagine that it has happened in the prehistory of the movie. Her guilt (about having lied about having had sex when she hadn't—can you imagine what the original Hester would think?) is just guilt-guilt and regret-regret, no fantastic flourishes or gorgeous luxuriance of fancy about it. While Emma Stone skulks around a California high school in strangely bedizened corsets (where do they come from? why are there so many?), she seems to take no real pleasure in doing so. I think the very point of *The Scarlet Letter* is that at least half of the pleasure (sexual and otherwise) to be found in the novel *is* the guilt.

The only thing I remember about my first, unsupervised reading of *The Scarlet Letter* is being surprised by the male name on the cover. I was surprised before I read it, because male-authored books so infrequently sported such intriguing bonnet-lady illustrations. But I was even more surprised after I read it, because it so expertly captured what I now recognize as the very femme sensibility I was cultivating.

Growing up with two brothers and mostly male friends, I wore my tomboy status as a badge of honor. I very publicly enjoyed horror movies and gangster rap. I broke into abandoned buildings to have a look around, trick rollerbladed (this may be the most embarrassing confession in this book), and camped in the woods without proper equipment. I refused makeup and dresses and heels, preferring the same oversized navy hoodie I wore for several years straight like a cloak of invisibility. But secretly, deep beneath my hoodied exterior, those bonnet fictions were defining me.

* * *

My guilty pleasure wasn't just reading lowbrow fiction or even female-authored fiction; it was being femme itself. (And throughout this book, I'll use the words "women," "femmes," and "femme-identified people" indiscriminately. A lot of different kinds of people are female.) From an early age, I associated my reading with my own femininity. It's no surprise really, because despite the very masculine nature of so-called highbrow literature, women have long been the keepers of literacy, and the reading of fiction more specifically, in America. Not only—according to 2017 Nielsen statistics—do 74 percent of American general-fiction readers identify as female, but, as the cultural historian Helen Taylor's research shows, women are also the majority of library patrons, book-club members, literary bloggers, and audiences at readings and literary festivals. Several times, and in different cities, I've taken my son to drag-queen reading hours. The children, in each case, were utterly rapt as the queens animated the stories they'd selected to read. Sitting on various weird-smelling rugs watching someone who probably fought very hard to express her femininity now share it through a love of reading, the femme power given to and derived from books became very clear to me.

When I was a child myself, the femme fictions I most cherished featured female protagonists who, like me, wrestled with their bookish tomboy status. "What are you reading," my older brother once asked me with a smirk, "another book about some gay girl who loves books?" At the time I was reading *The Story Girl*, the L. M. Montgomery classic about an unconventional, charismatic young woman who loves books and storytelling more than fresh sea air or new ribbons or even strawberry preserves! That is, in fact, what all Montgomery books are about. The story girl was awesome. And she gets the guy, too— dreamy Peter falls for her over the much prettier and more conventionally femme Felicity, all through the ultimate (and oft-underestimated) power of telling tales. I think, in retrospect, this appealed to me not because I harbored a fantasy of seducing the objects of my crushes through tale-telling (this hardly seemed a possibility, especially as my crushes tended to be on people to whom I never spoke) but because such plots fused a love of books with an embrace of femme desires—for sexual objects but for other (often embroidered) pleasures too. I didn't really associate with or envy the overtly femme girls like Felicity in my own world—the ones who carried handbags to school instead of backpacks and wore silver charm bracelets and were versed in the mysteries of hairstyling with heat tools and note-passing with boyfriends—but I didn't see myself as fundamentally different from them either. I understood at some level that my femmeness was to be found in my fictions, not my accessories. It was safer that way.

To be out-and-out femme seemed somehow too bold or too dangerous. It would have been a liability to advertise my femininity in my male-dominated family or among the male friends who treated me as a brother in their band. The magazines I read alongside my books—titles like *Teen* and *YM*—taught me that to be female was a condition of perpetual shame and embarrassment. My favorite feature in *Teen* was called "Why Me?"—an entrant in a full-fledged 1990s genre including *YM*'s "Say Anything" and *Seventeen*'s "Traumarama." These regular columns were not dissimilar to *Penthouse*'s "Forum," but rather than epistolary fantasies of improbable sexual scenarios, they consisted of letters sent in by young women who had endured unthinkable catastrophes of social humiliation. In my recollection, about 85 percent of these involved some strange set of circumstances wherein it became publicly revealed that the letter writer was, in fact, a menstruating woman. Whether a stain on the back of her jeans when called to write on the blackboard or a male friend overhearing her ask his mom for a pad, these indignities seemed like radical confessions of a dark shared secret. I cherished them.

One letter in particular I will never forget: the heartfelt epistle of a young woman who decided that the safest place to hide a spare menstrual product on a school canoe trip was under her hat. When her hat fell off in a particularly choppy part of the water, she knew everyone could see the pad that remained perfectly balanced atop her head, its adhesive strip stuck in her hair. She could not remove it with her hands for fear of losing her oars to the current, so had to endure her entire class—even the boys!—gazing at the vision of her rowing past wearing an Always like a crown. Clearly, this tale raises far more questions than it answers, but I think therein lies its greatness. The utter absurdity of the plot exposes the absurdity of the impossible contradictions of women's lives: the constant struggle to be an object of desire with no desire to someone you desire, to be disembodied but rivetingly beautiful to look at, to walk gracefully in tall, uncomfortable shoes and do great and powerful things without threatening the egos of the men who demand that you do them. The truest tales of womanhood are always outlandish; to be female in our culture is, in itself, such a ludicrous proposition.

What is *The Scarlet Letter: A Romance* (that's the subtitle) but a long, baroque "Why Me?" letter that begins, *So once my husband sent me to live with the Puritans in the new world*? It spoke to me in the same way *The Story Girl* and the Anne books and Judy Blume did. Femaleness is synonymous with shame, these stories said. Desire with humiliation. Pleasure with guilt. Among these texts, only *The Scarlet Letter* gets to be a required-reading "classic." And look, we could debate this, but I know the score: it's a classic in large part because the person who wrote it was male.

The nineteenth-century American books I was assigned in high school were all written by men: Hawthorne, Emerson, Thoreau, Melville. But these were not the books that most nineteenth-century Americans were reading. Melville sold about 35,000 copies of *all* of his books while he was alive, making roughly $10,000 in lifetime earnings for his writing. *The Scarlet Letter*, Hawthorne's most commercially successful work, sold less than 8,000 copies in his lifetime, making him only $1,500. The best-selling single book of the nineteenth century was Harriet Beecher Stowe's *Uncle Tom's Cabin*, a work that sold 310,000 copies in America in the first year it was released (making Stowe $10,000 in the first three months alone) and went on to be translated into multiple languages—selling over two million copies by 1857. Augusta Jane Wilson's *St. Elmo* (1866) was read by an estimated one million people in the first four months after its publication. And the best-selling author of the nineteenth century overall was a woman named E.D.E.N. Southworth, who wrote anywhere from fifty to seventy novels (scholars are not quite sure) that sold hundreds of thousands of copies each, making her a staggering $10,000 a year in royalties—about $200,000 in today's money. That's a decent living.

In a now-infamous 1855 letter that Hawthorne wrote to his publisher, William Ticknor, he complained, "America is now wholly given over to a d[amne]d mob of scribbling women, and I should have no chance of success while the public is occupied with their trash." So, while he wrote a guilty pleasure novel himself, he also kind of defined the guilty pleasure genre by calling books written by women "trash." Which is to say, he implied that the popular novels selling like hotcakes were bad not only because they had melodramatic plots about being in love and in danger and in love with the men who put them in danger (basically the plot of *The Scarlet Letter*) but because they were both about women and written by women. He felt guilty about being an unsuccessful femme writer, and he took it out on the badass bonnet-wearers who were actually getting it done.

What's amazing is that after all of these years, the terms "guilty pleasure" and "trash" or "trashy" media still signify as female. Guilty pleasures are often critically framed as equal opportunity. And it's true that all kinds of people are narcissistically obsessed with both cultivating their tastes and figuring out ways to violate them. But an online search for "#guiltypleasure" quickly reveals that the genres that get tagged this way (romantic comedies, soap operas, romance novels, competitive reality TV, HGTV, pop music by female solo artists) are typically by, about, and for women. In our current post-postmodern moment, omnivorousness in taste has a certain vogue. Yet this cultural development has somehow strengthened, rather than undone, the gendered ideological force of this way of classifying what we consume for the sheer enjoyment of the thing. It's charming for a highbrow male music critic to express an unbidden passion for Taylor Swift or Carly Rae Jepsen, but, for a female critic, the stakes of making such a confession are somewhat higher. The subjects of guiltily pleasurable media—stories about falling for a questionable man (e.g., *Bridget Jones*, *Fifty Shades*), stories about the vertiginous return home of a fancy business lady (nearly all Hallmark holiday movies and also some films with bigger names like Holly Hunter, Reese Witherspoon, and Sandra Bullock), stories about girls trying to be grown up (*The Baby-Sitters Club*), stories about women who become girls or girls who become women (*Freaky Friday*, *13 Going on 30*, *Never Been Kissed*, or *Little*), as well as every Selena Gomez song, home-makeover reality shows, fashion-makeover reality shows, etc.—share a fixation on the experience of being out of place or (at the level of behavior, embodiment, or desire) out of social alignment. This overwhelming preoccupation with the experience of being humiliated, dominated, or even abused has long pervaded the stories that make up women's culture—from eighteenth-century epistolary novels about women who literally die because they fall in love out of wedlock all the way to "Why Me?" and beyond.

The pad-on-the-head embarrassment of reading a romance novel in many circles is only slightly more agonizing than that of being caught listening to Taylor Swift (this is changing somewhat recently, pace her collaborations with "serious" musicians like Bon Iver and Ryan Adams' cover album), or watching *Sex and the City* or anything starring Hilary Duff. Jane Anne Krentz, a best-selling romance novelist herself, writes in the introduction to *Dangerous Men and Adventurous Women*, "Few people realize how much courage it takes for a woman to open a romance novel on an airplane. . . . [Society] labels the books as trash and the readers as unintelligent, uneducated, unsophisticated, or neurotic . . . [yet] the person who does not like to read horror or science fiction is unlikely to criticize the genres or chastise and condemn the readers who do love them." There are plenty of guilty pleasure genres that don't have to do with being female per se: boy bands, slow jams, celebrity news, processed foods. But maybe all of these things do have a femme sensibility about them, if only because the construct "guilty pleasure" is itself a descriptor of what it feels like to be female.

"Femininity, as an idea, *does* fuck you up," Hilton Als writes in *White Girls*, as a way of describing the impact white women had on the formation of his own identity. And while I agree that all femmes do get fucked up by the patriarchy, I think that pathologizing them for the consequences of this external oppression is ill-advised. Being fucked up is not the worst way to come into an identity, and having been fucked up should not preclude us from enjoying the forms of media that speak to that experience. Absorbing femme fictions as I have for my entire life has not been an experience of self-flagellation, nor have I spent my years prescribing myself tales of feminine submission as penance for the sins of being a woman. In fact, the opposite is true. Seeing these stories enacted has been profoundly liberating—not in the sense that they liberated me from the patriarchy or even from my own significant fuckedupedness. What they did instead was to offer a very powerful form of love: the feeling of being seen. They reminded me that my fantasies aren't strange and my insecurities aren't idiosyncratic. They validated every humiliating desire.

This is not the typical take on cultural documents of female humiliation. For example, the critic Carly Moore writes, "On the surface, 'Traumarama!' stories seem to provide readers with real stories about imperfect girls, but because the girls in these stories are so severely punished for being real and imperfect, the benefits are lost. These stories, in fact, tell girls that it is not okay to be real or imperfect, even if they learn that many girls feel similarly," condemning the shame columns of my youth for recapitulating the sexist messages of the culture. But for me, this is precisely why they were valuable and cathartic to read. In depicting that shame, they acknowledged its realness. In the culture in which I was raised, it *wasn't* okay for girls to be real or imperfect. To pretend otherwise would have been to disregard what suffering inside of that reality was really like.

There's a debate that goes around the (almost entirely female) academic circles that study the texts Hawthorne referred to as having been written by "the damned mob of scribbling women" that goes something like this: Were these women subversively protesting the heterosexist, oppressive world they depicted *by* depicting it? Or did such depictions only more rigidly enforce heterosexist norms? I've never had red hair and freckles, but I've always wondered what I'd think of *Anne of Green Gables* if I did. Anne is deeply ashamed of her physical characteristics and tends to blame every life disappointment on these supposedly wanting aspects of her appearance. One way to ask the big question the aforementioned debate poses is this: Does Anne teach those who have red hair and freckles to be ashamed of them—or does she make them proud to see their own freckle-shame lodged just as deep in the breast of their intrepid heroine? I'm guessing it's the latter.

Personally, I would like to see the entire heteropatriarchy burned so far down to the ground that we have to make use of apocalyptic seed banks to regrow food and must spend several years walking around a moody, ash-strewn wasteland, and yet I also love these guilty pleasures with all my heart. I love E.D.E.N. Southworth's *The Hidden Hand* and Susan Warner's *The Wide, Wide World*. I love the Netflix teen romcom *To All the Boys I've Loved Before*, I love *Bridget Jones's Diary* and *Romy and Michele's High School Reunion*. I love *Gossip Girl* and *Downton Abbey* and nearly every BBC adaptation of a Jane Austen novel ever made. I love Selena Gomez's music as much as I love her movies (hugely but with very few notable exceptions). Alone in the car on a desolate stretch of highway, I've brought myself to tears singing Natalie Imbruglia's "Torn" as though the fate of my life hung in the balance.

Great works in the canon of guilty pleasures reveal how, through indulging the guilt attendant to the second-class status to which femme subjects have long been relegated, readers and viewers are free, as Alan Watts suggests in the epigraph to this chapter, to continue to not do anything about it. Watts means that in a critical way, like Brené Brown—as though we should be actively doing something to ameliorate the situation of our guilt. But Watts may not have considered that some kinds of guilt come from circumstances, like being female, about which there's often very little one can—or wants to—do.

These kinds of guilt need only catharsis. Like Hester's scarlet letter that is both her punishment and her passion, these guilty pleasures offer a particularly femme catharsis. The domination they depict, abstractly, by the society in which they're set (ours), but also directly, by the men who so often play in their love plots (who leave their heroines "torn"), is a part of their appeal. It's very possible to be both against such domination in real life and deeply into it in more imaginary spaces. If to be female is to be guilty, then the fantasy of domination is an absolution from that guilt, experienced as pleasure.

And so this book is not about taste or aesthetic shame. Rather, it is about the specifically pleasurable forms of feminine shame and guilt stimulated by supposedly "lowbrow" aesthetic tendencies. In three chapters that follow the arc of femme fictions themselves, ("Rough Sex," "Expensive Sheets," and "Saying Yes to the Dress"), this book tells the story of the libidinal and base desires that guilty pleasures help many femmes experience. These are often incoherent desires: for corsets and powerlessness; for money, high-thread-count sheets, and white privilege; for the specifically femme power that the wedding dress—the pièce de résistance of patriarchy—represents. While there's undoubtedly something wrong with the culture that produces these desires, there's absolutely nothing wrong with the person who experiences them, even revels in them. To suggest that such desires are bad—or ought to intensify their consumer's guilt for the very act of consuming them—is to blame the victim of cultural circumstance. She may fight with all her power to overthrow the oppressive conditions of our culture, but it is already inside of her. To shame the consumption of these cultural objects is to make women responsible for the conditions of their own oppression, to continue to deny pleasure to subjects for whom the denial of pleasure is already a birthright.

1

ROUGH SEX

> I'm all out of faith
> This is how I feel
> I'm cold and I am shamed
> Lying naked on the floor
> Illusion never changed
> Into something real
> I'm wide awake and I can see the perfect sky
> is torn
> —Natalie Imbruglia, "Torn"

Trained exactly where to bend at the spine, the used romance novel found in a bookstore or at a beach-house rental will almost always open on its own to the sexiest pages. Most readers of romance novels—the most quintessential guilty pleasure genre—skip right to the sexy bits. It's true that I'm prone to absolutes, but I also think it highly likely that *all* rereaders of romance novels return to those passages first. So I forgive you if you choose to skip to the long quotations included herein; or you could bear with me through this chapter about the cultural history of the rough-sex fictions we call "bodice-rippers"—explicitly sexual romance novels primarily set in the nineteenth century—and why femme readers so love them.

It's no coincidence that the twentieth-century second coming of the nineteenth-century romance is often set in the nineteenth century. Present-day people tend to associate the Regency and Victorian eras with retrogressive gender politics, despite the fact that many of the issues raised in the nineteenth-century women's movement are still entirely unresolved today. (The ladies of the 1850s, no less than women today, were very much clear that *we need to do something about child support and rape culture*, ahem.) If the nineteenth century is the imagined primal scene of gendered oppression for modern women—conjuring images of corsets and confinement—it's no surprise that the books in which the corsets are ripped off and the sex that was previously only a vague fantasy is made real are so cathartic to so many readers.

Though we know them as bodice-rippers, I've always thought these books might as well be called bonnet-tossers because, for me, the bonnet is a far more potent symbol of the female shame and guilt that the desire to be really, deeply fucked is about ripping through or tossing off. I like it, of course, when the bodice comes off. It's good, too, when the petticoat is lifted and the stockings unbuckled. But nothing beats the tantalizing possibilities of a bonnet and all it signifies.

Bonnets are important to what I'm interested in here because it's in the bonnet, more than the corset or the petticoat, that we can connect from sex back to shame. If the "Why Me?" / "Traumarama" columns of my youth were both cathartic forum and conduct manual for people on the cusp of womanhood in the early 1990s such as myself, the female-authored sentimental novels of the nineteenth century provided my bonnet-wearing counterparts a similar service. I think the fact that bonnets were such a clear signifier of shame is what attracted me to stories about women wearing them.

Like a pad on the head, the bonnet is an obvious sign of female, secondary status. Bonnet-wearing was mandatory throughout most of the nineteenth century in England and North America, though bonnets were only worn outside and therefore for the benefit of others. Bonnets, ostensibly there for "decency" or protection, remind their wearers that they have bodies they ought to be deeply humiliated about. Women wore bonnets because it would have been shameful to appear without them, but the bonnets were also a constant reminder of the shame of being female itself. As the literary critic and clothing historian Daneen Wardrop writes, "no item of apparel can be more socially overt than the bonnet, no item so close, literally, to the thoughts of the wearer."

Practically every woman I know who is a scholar of nineteenth-century fiction had a childhood obsession with bonnets—one even confessed to me that she had her mother sew her her very own bonnet, which, adorably, she wore when she read. Clothing historians lose their shit over bonnets because they are the best indicators of microchanges in fashion. While a new dress would be a very expensive article to come by indeed, new bonnets or at the very least new bonnet trimmings were relatively easy to manage. So there was little to no excuse to be behind the times in bonnets unless you were really out to lunch, fashion-wise. Because of this, an unfashionable bonnet would be a source of great shame to its wearer.

Even nineteenth-century women themselves saw the humor and pathos in bonnet-wearing. Wardrop writes a whole chapter about the vicissitudes of Emily Dickinson's relationship to the bonnets of her friends and family members, recounting numerous hilarious bonnet-bashing letters written by Dickinson (girl could be *catty* about a bonnet) and a chilling moment when "[Dickinson's] reactions crystallize into a few dire and haunting sentences about her own bonnet." Such passages leave me delightedly bereaved.

One of my own favorite bonnet scenes happens near the beginning of Susan Warner's 1850 novel *The Wide, Wide World*. It takes place on a carriage journey to the boat that will take the protagonist, Ellen, far away from her beloved mother for the first time. In this already-vulnerable circumstance, the mean girls in the carriage mock Ellen because she is wearing the wrong bonnet. Not only is (obviously) having the wrong bonnet on your head an utterly terrible fate for a nineteenth-century girl to endure, but what's worse is that Ellen doesn't even know why they're making fun of her at first: "She did not know that her white bonnet was such a matter of merriment to Margaret Dunscombe and the maid, that they could hardly contain themselves." Agony. When she finally does hear them openly mocking her bonnet aboard the ship, she runs into the empty saloon and rips the "despised bonnet" off her head in a "burst of her indignation." It would be an overstatement to say that I cry when I read this scene, but not much of one.

Ellen's despised bonnet represents the vulnerability of her circumstance. She is almost entirely uneducated in the ways of conduct and fashion. The opposite of a woman of the "wide, wide world," Ellen is a clueless young girl unwillingly thrust into that world. And a significant part of her problem is that she has no tools to use to figure out how much social and physical danger she is in at any given time, how she ought to behave, or even whether she has already made a potentially irreversible misstep. In the absence of her mother, she has to trust other women to guide her in her quest. The structure of Ellen's adventures kind of resembles a video game wherein the object is to get to her wedding while avoiding all the bosses who threaten her along the way—bad men who will rape her, mean girls who will shame her, and countless social pitfalls that stand to spoil her chances of ever finding bodily and financial safety in the form of a husband. Of course, I do not see my own life in this way, nor do I particularly understand Ellen as a nineteenth-century analog of myself. But she is a character cast in a mold that still existed in the culture of my youth—a mold that still exists today. She is a girl trying to figure out what this whole being-a-woman-in-a-patriarchal-world thing means, and she gets a lot of mixed messages.

Another problem with this quest of Ellen's—to find a husband in order to secure her future well-being—is that she seems wholly unaware she's on it. This is part of the mold she must fit into. The Cult of True Womanhood is what historians call the nineteenth-century ideology that a woman ought to be pious, submissive, domestic, and pure. In other words, she must cherish God above all else, defer to the wisdom and power of men, be an angel in the home who makes life for the male folk around her more comfortable and pleasant, and not get busy with anyone but her future husband—only after they are married, of course. Like the history of wars that leaves out what everyone else was doing, novels that subscribe to the Cult of True Womanhood (and *The Wide, Wide World* certainly is one) outline a particular kind of story but also color outside those lines just a bit. Keen readers are rewarded with a sense of what is not being explicitly depicted.

Women are often keen readers of texts because we've long been trained in interpretation and analysis through the conditions of our lives. We have to read the subtle clues about what to do in circumstances that arise while having a female body, circumstances we've been made uncomfortable to discuss openly, such as those that involve sexual harassment, reproductive health, sexual pleasure, and the stunning array of cultural expectations we're expected to uphold as daughters, mothers, workers, girlfriends, wives, and members of our communities. Perhaps a more accurate description of what happens in *The Wide, Wide World* is that we come to understand more about the dimensions of Ellen's life than she herself is allowed to acknowledge, given the constraints of her culture. To be successful as a character, she has to remain in a state of perpetual ignorance. This is not dissimilar from how women today often have to pretend ignorance or guilelessness in order to achieve our desired ends. (How many times have I listened to an appliance repairman or auto mechanic or hardware-store employee explain things to me that mostly every adult human being already knows because I wanted him to simply fix a thing and I cannot dude-bro with him about it without causing social friction and potentially incurring additional financial cost to myself because, you know, to quote Gwen Stefani, "I'm just a girl in the world, that's all that you'll let me be"?)

The need to be or to appear pure was so crucial to obtaining the ultimate mark of nineteenth-century female success—a good marriage—that in order to land the husband, women like Ellen had to pretend to be as uninterested in men as I pretend to be in home repair (I'm very interested!), to the point of not even thinking about courtship or marriage. How do you work through the preliminaries, then? Well, let's look at the scene where Ellen meets her love interest, John, the man that every reader can easily see she will eventually marry. First, some context: after the disastrous bonnet incident, Ellen ends up living with her aunt, a gruff spinster named Fortune who owns and runs her own farm, wears comfortable clothing, and is "good-looking and smart"—all of which people in the neighborhood find "queer" because they're terrible. Since Ellen can't learn Cult of True Womanhood stuff from the system-defying Aunt Fortune, she befriends an angelic neighbor named Alice. Ellen and Alice spend a lot of time discussing how to be a good Christian, a good domestic, a good submissive—you know, girl stuff. Through the intimacy forged over this tutelage, Ellen and Alice decide that they are sisters.* Alice adores her older brother John, whom she tells Ellen all about in his absence. Then John finally

---

* NB: The feminist theorist Gayle Rubin once signed a letter "yours in embittered sisterhood," which is just a casual acknowledgment away from this early phase of women gaming the patriarchy. Perhaps you are familiar with the "Bechdel test"—a very good metric invented by the graphic novelist Allison Bechdel for illustrating the weak representation of women in film. Bechdel asks that, for the proper and equitable representation of women, a film must have a conversation between two female characters about something other than men. My one complaint about this test is that it implies that talking about men is some kind of antifeminist activity, whereas I actually see most of my conversations about men with other women in the same vein as Alice and Ellen's: they are strategizing about managing the overlords!

comes back home, and Alice introduces them, which creates a truly creepy moment wherein John makes Ellen give him a kiss because it is his "brother's right."

Even though there's a social prohibition on such displays between men and women generally, casting John as Ellen's pseudobrother via her relationship with Alice makes it okay to kiss him and hang out with him one-on-one, which they often do. But right there in the same passage, at that first meeting, the brother-cover is pretty much blown because we also get that she's actively desirous of him in a very unsisterly way. Here's the next bit: "Ellen's eyes sought the stranger as if by fascination. She watched him whenever she could without being noticed. At first she was in doubt what to think of him; she was quite sure from that one look into his eyes that he was a person to be feared; there was no doubt of that, as to the rest she didn't know." It's John's very scariness that tips us off to the fact that she covertly thinks he's sexy. This continues throughout the whole book. In a later scene, John comes up in conversation with the girls in the village when Ellen is having some trouble controlling her new pony. We've all been there, right?

But seriously, I probably needn't explain to you the sexual dimensions of the young-female obsession with horses. Horse books for girls are as clearly about the discovery of one's own sexuality as muscle cars are for aging men. Sometimes, in these books, the girl is the horse (see Mary O'Hara's *My Friend Flicka* [1943]), sometimes she's the rider (see Marguerite Henry's *Misty of Chincoteague* [1947], especially where Maureen is "unaware of everything but a sharp ecstasy" while "riding her mount"). These texts tap into the young-femme need to "tame" her own sexual desire and to negotiate the complex power dynamics that she knows, on some level, heterosexual sex will entail. Anyhow, in *The Wide, Wide World*, Ellen's girlfriends suggest she needs to whip her pony to make it behave:

"Whip him!" said Ellen, "I don't want to whip him, I am sure; and I should be afraid to besides."

"Hasn't John taught you that lesson yet?" said the young lady; "he is perfect in it himself. Do you remember, Alice, the chastising he gave that fine black horse of ours we called the 'Black Prince'?—a beautiful creature he was—more than a year ago? My conscience! he frightened me to death."

"I remember," said Alice; "I remember I could not look on."

"What did he do that for?" said Ellen.

"What's the matter, Ellen Montgomery?" said Miss Sophia, laughing, "where did you get that long face from? Are you thinking of John or the horse?"

Ellen's eye turned to Alice.

"My dear Ellen," said Alice, smiling, though she spoke seriously, "it was necessary; it sometimes is necessary to do such things. You do not suppose John would do it cruelly or unnecessarily?"

Ellen's face shortened considerably. . . .

"A very determined 'use,'" said Miss Sophia. "I advise you, Ellen, not to trust your pony to Mr. John; he'll have no mercy on him."

The critic Marianne Noble brilliantly read the erotics of this scene in her 2000 book *The Masochistic Pleasures of Sentimental Literature*, arguing that Ellen—a devout Protestant who believes in God's loving discipline, turning the other cheek, etc.—associates punishment with love and therefore desires a partner who excels at discipline. His skill at training horses, Noble argues, translates into Ellen's desire to be trained by him. Ellen wants to be the pony, and she wants him to take no mercy on her. Noble writes that "if [John's] discipline is painful that is all the better, since Ellen empirically knows that pain can produce pleasure." This reading, built on the theories of masochism advanced by sexologists and theorists ranging from Alfred Kinsey to Jessica Benjamin to Jacques Lacan to Michel Foucault, associates the sexual appeal of domination with the experience of physical pain.

Pain is an intense sensation. If you associate pain with love, then when you're in intense pain, you feel an intensity of love. Makes sense. But I've always read this scene as Ellen being more excited by the erotics of humiliation than by the erotics of physical pain—partly because the scene is not just about punishment but about punishment being witnessed and evaluated. The kind of punishment all women, including the fictional Ellen, receive repeatedly and consistently throughout their lives is a microaggressive shaming at the hands of people of all genders utterly steeped in patriarchal culture. Women's fictions are almost always about this. The witch on the pyre or the A embroidered on the dress are extreme examples of slut shaming, but there are other and subtler kinds of shaming as well. And often this shame is a double bind.

Consider the issue of makeup. In the Amazon streaming show *The Marvelous Mrs. Maisel*, the title character refuses to allow her husband to see her without it and so waits until he is asleep to remove it and awakes before him to reapply it. My own Jewish, Brooklyn-bred grandmother did this exact thing and frequently expressed her horror at my insistence on appearing in public without "my face on"—a phrase that has long stuck with me in its beautiful implication that the face you create with your makeup is the true face you put forward to the world and your unvarnished face a mere draft of a face, some embarrassingly unfinished work not to be aired publicly. I can think of nothing so richly symbolic of what it feels like to be a femme subject than to be compelled to cover the site of your face—to identify with a mask over your own body.

And yet, at the same time, there is a reverse prohibition *against* wearing makeup. When the academic blogger and professional academic career adviser Karen Kelsky announced a series about wearing makeup in her blog *The Professor Is In* in 2017, she couched her topic in highly defensive language that is completely understandable given that there is a long-standing tradition of women in professional academic roles appearing without, as my grandmother would say, their faces on: "If you feel strongly that makeup is a tool of the patriarchy," she writes, "I hear you, and I understand where you're coming from. However, I don't agree with that as a blanket statement. I believe that makeup can be for some people a means of self-care and creative expression that is both empowering and pleasurable. . . . I will not engage with makeup-shaming here or on any Facebook or Twitter comment threads." "Makeup-shaming" is, it is perhaps needless to say, a thing because the makeup-wearing woman supposedly communicates her loyal subjecthood to the patriarchal order. So in some contexts it is shameful to appear without makeup (say, a formal wedding or a first date), while in others (an academic job interview or an athletic competition) it might be a shameful sign of your "unseriousness" to appear with it.

This constant need to shape the self in response to the demands of the given social situation is daunting, exhausting, and can sometimes feel downright terrifying—especially because, like Ellen in the carriage with her bonnet, no one ever tells you! I have always thought, in the midst of this tyranny, that it's kinder to inform your sister about the lipstick on her teeth or that her skirt is tucked into her tights or that her blouse has become undone to reveal her bra because the only thing worse than having to pretend to have flawless (and therefore nonexistent) bodies is receiving so precious little help in figuring out how to pull off this illusion. Additionally, such gestures create an acknowledgment of the female body in a supportive context—a rare thing indeed.

* * *

The moment when a female person is being shamed for having a body is just about the only time the existence of that body is truly acknowledged. Those teen-magazine columns that shed so much ink on the humiliation of revealing the fact of menstruation were some of the only places I found in girlhood where it was textually acknowledged that women menstruate! Another place was season 2, episode 1, of *The Golden Girls*—"The Curse," where Blanche becomes convinced she is no longer a woman because she's begun to go through menopause at the same time the "girls" have decided to start a side hustle as mink breeders (clearly worth a rewatch). I see this text as a companion piece to a little book by Judy Blume called *Are You There God? It's Me, Margaret"* (1970), wherein the protagonist struggles simultaneously with identifying her spiritual orientation toward the world and managing her profound desire to become a woman by getting her period. These texts told me a lot of things as a child, but here are two biggies: (1) that women are defined and valued by their ability to reproduce and (2) that though the ability to reproduce is the single most valuable proposition of womanhood, the conditions of the female body that indicate that ability are not to be openly discussed because they are a subject of great shame. *Fear your limited power*, they say. *Hide your body, your strength.*

Blume is a master depicter of female body shame, which is a primary reason why her books have been so resonant with so many people. In *Deenie* (1973), the shame comes in the form of the title character's scoliosis, which causes her to have to wear a brace. The brace is the corrective—the external appendage that will fix the imperfections of her spine—but also, like my grandmother's "face," it follows the shape of her body to become one with it. When the boy she has a crush on, Buddy, pulls her into the laundry room to make out with her, he asks if she can take off the brace:

> Buddy grabbed my hand and led me to the part of the basement where Janet's mother does the laundry. It was dark and kind of damp in there and smelled like Clorox. Buddy said, "Couldn't you take off your brace for a little while?"
>
> I thought about the shopping bag I'd left upstairs. "No," I told Buddy. "I have to wear it all the time."
>
> "Oh well . . ." Buddy said. This time when he kissed me I concentrated on kissing him back. I hoped I was doing it right.

This passage reads to me like a poem on the subject of female guilt and shame. The details make it—from the location in the dark, damp laundry room (where grown women laboriously cover the traces of the body with the punishing scent and bleaching power of Clorox) to the abandoned shopping bag (the symbol of female desires left behind) to the experience of kissing being one centered on the pleasure of the other rather than the self. But the real revolutionary moment here is Deenie's response to Buddy's request. "No," she tells him, "I have to wear it all the time." On one level, what I want to see here is Deenie ripping off the brace, grabbing Buddy in her arms, and telling him to go to town. But in some ways that would be much less than what we get, which is an acknowledgment that one's brace must be worn *All. The. Time.* You see, even if Deenie literally took it off, figuratively it would still be there, and any sex act that failed to acknowledge its presence would be both untrue and unsatisfying. To love her, he must love both the body and the brace. Psychically, they are the same.

When the laughing Miss Sophia asks Ellen, "Are you thinking of John or the horse?" the answer must be both. The pairing is a way of acknowledging the simultaneity of the experience of erotic desire with the shame at having it: the desire to be a sexually expressive being and the desire to have one's sexuality tamed or suppressed. Ellen's sexual longing for

John includes the acknowledgment of her shame at experiencing that longing. The fantasy of rough sex with him (which, I think, along with Noble, all of this horsewhipping talk clearly implies) is a fantasy of the release of two pressures: pent-up desires and pent-up humiliation.

John is a clergyman in the streets but a horsewhipper in the sheets: a good man with a violent streak. There's a reason why this kind of guy has become a cultural cliché who emerges in the form of the detective with a troubled past, the cowboy with a temper, the murderous Scottish Highlander with a love of family, or the gentlemanly vampire. His violence is both the threat and the shelter. As the present-day singer King Princess croons, "I don't care if you degrade me, 'cause after all you are my safety." The truth of the matter is, someone is going to whip Ellen's pony. Better for it to be John.

Nineteenth-century sentimental novels abound with this guy, whom cultural historians of romance novels like Pamela Regis call "the dark hero." In E.D.E.N. Southworth's 1859 novel *The Hidden Hand*, he is the villain rather than the brother-suitor, but just as John's scariness tips us off to Ellen's desire for him, the passages describing the villainous Black Donald reek of the heroine Capitola's passion for him and what he represents. When Capitola asks her housekeeper about him after overhearing his name, he is immediately associated with sexual violence:

"Who is Black Donald? Good gracious, child, you ask me who is Black Donald!"

"Yes; who is he? where is he? what is he? that every cheek turns pale at the mention of his name?" asked Capitola.

"Black Donald! Oh, my child, may you never know more of Black Donald than I can tell you. Black Donald is the chief of a band of ruthless desperadoes that infest these mountain roads, robbing mail coaches, stealing negroes, breaking into houses and committing every sort of depredation. Their hands are red with murder and their souls black with darker crimes."

"Darker crimes than murder!" ejaculated Capitola.

"Yes, child, yes; there are darker crimes. Only last winter he and three of his gang broke into a solitary house where there was a lone woman and her daughter, and—it is not a story for you to hear; but if the people had caught Black Donald then they would have burned him at the stake! His life is forfeit by a hundred crimes. He is an outlaw, and a heavy price is set upon his head."

"And can no one take him?"

"No, my dear; at least, no one has been able to do so yet. His very haunts are unknown, but are supposed to be in concealed mountain caverns."

"How I would like the glory of capturing Black Donald!" said Capitola.

Capitola is quite figuratively "ejaculating" over Donald's "darker crimes" here, and her desire to "capture" him becomes even clearer once we receive a physical description of him:

> Black Donald, from his great stature, might have been a giant walked out of the age of fable into the middle of the nineteenth century. From his stature alone, he might have been chosen leader of this band of desperadoes. He stood six feet eight inches in his boots, and was stout and muscular in proportion. He had a well-formed, stately head, fine aquiline features, dark complexion, strong, steady, dark eyes, and an abundance of long curling black hair and beard that would have driven to despair a Broadway beau, broken the heart of a Washington belle, or made his own fortune in any city of America as a French count or a German baron! He had decidedly "the air noble and distinguished."

I'd like to pause a moment and reflect on the fact that he is six feet eight. Even by today's standards, that is absurdly tall. Then, pray, a second moment for his hair. You can really only imagine this guy as Mandy Patinkin in *The Princess Bride* meets 1970s Tom Selleck in real life, meets Johnny Depp in *Pirates of the Caribbean*, meets how you and I both feel about Jason Momoa at any given time. In fact, I think if you read *The Hidden Hand* imagining Jason Momoa in the role of Black Donald, its messages become crystalline.

When Capitola and Black Donald finally do meet, he is as captivated with her as she is with him. He tells his band of robbers in their hidden lair that she is "such a girl! slender, petite, lithe, with bright, black ringlets dancing around a little face full of fun, frolic, mischief and spirit, and bright eyes quick and vivacious as those of a monkey." This monkey-eyed Capitola is his feminine double—equally black ring-leted and mischievous and as small and fragile as he is large and indestructible. Their physical difference conjures a fantasy of erotic submission, and indeed, when Capitola first tries to "capture" him, by jumping on his enormous back, the narrator reflects, "He could have killed her instantly in any one of a dozen ways. He could have driven in her temples with a blow of his sledge-hammer fist; he could have broken her neck with the grip of his iron fingers; he only wished to shake her off without hurting her"—this is that same tantalizing shelter/threat combo we get from John: he could kill her, but he doesn't want to. He gives up his power to destroy her for the love of her. This is a fantasy of domination but also of acceptance and safety.

Toward the end of the novel, Black Donald sneaks into Capitola's bed chamber. Once she realizes that he's locked them in there together and that there would be no one to hear her screams if he attacked her, she acknowledges, "She was, therefore, entirely in the power of Black Donald." She decides to trick him into submission by convincing him she's not afraid of him, and the following flirty dialogue ensues:

"Afraid of you? No, I guess not!" replied Cap, with a toss of her head.

"Yet, I might do you some harm."

"But, you won't!"

"Why won't I?"

"Because it won't pay!"

"Why wouldn't it?"

"Because you couldn't do me any harm, unless you were to kill me, and you would gain nothing by my death, except a few trinkets that you may have without."

"Then, you are really not afraid of me?" he asked, taking another deep draught of brandy. . . .

"No, indeed! I liked you, long before I ever saw you! I always did like people that make other people's hair stand on end! Don't you remember when you first came here disguised as a peddler, though I did not know who you were, when we were talking of Black Donald, and everybody was abusing him, except myself? I took his part and said that for my part I liked Black Donald and wanted to see him."

"Sure enough, my jewel, so you did! And didn't I bravely risk my life by throwing off my disguise to gratify your laudable wish?"

"So you did, my hero!"

"Ah, but well as you liked me, the moment you thought me in your power didn't you leap upon my shoulders like a catamount and cling there, shouting to all the world to come and help you, for you had caught Black Donald and would die before you would give him up? Ah! you little vampire, how you thirsted for my blood! And you pretended to like me!" said Black Donald, eying her from head to foot, with a sly leer.

Cap returned the look with interest. Dropping her head on one side, she glanced upward from the corner of her eye, with an expression of "infinite" mischief and roguery, saying "Lor, didn't you know why I did that?"

"Because you wanted me captured, I suppose."

"No, indeed, but, because—"

"Well, what?"

"Because I wanted you to carry me off!"

"Well, I declare! I never thought of that!" said the outlaw, dropping his bread and cheese, and staring at the young girl.

"Well, you might have thought of it then! I was tired of hum-drum life, and I wanted to see adventures!" said Cap.

Black Donald looked at the mad girl from head to foot and then said, coolly: "Miss Black. I am afraid you are not good."

Capitola's "ruse" to trick Black Donald into submission reveals the nature of her true feelings about him. Is she dissembling when she says that she likes him or that she wanted him to carry her off? It's as difficult to believe there is no truth to these "lies" as it is to believe Ellen always thinks of John as a brother. Capitola is *not* good—in the sense that she is neither pious nor pure nor submissive nor domestic. She wants Black Donald not only because he looks like Jason Momoa but also because he represents social disturbance. A wanted criminal who lives communally with his band of outlaws, he is an anarchistic element in the corrupt system that forces her to be ashamed and obedient.

Like the disobedient stallion that might throw you to your death but also feels pretty damn good to ride, the dark hero is a figure of both female oppression and its release. While sentimental novels became popular by alluding to the dark-hero fantasy with various degrees of subtlety and misdirection, that same figure became a staple of the twentieth-century popular romance—and in these texts, the sex that was only implied between the plucky heroines of the previous century and their dark, troubled heroes became *very* explicitly depicted.

* * *

When I was growing up, everyone's mom seemed to have a bath-water-logged romance novel tucked alongside the *National Geographic*s in the bathroom magazine holder. I honestly never read romance novels as a kid, which is a shame because I obviously would have loved them. If I had read them rather than flipping through the exploitative pictures of foreign women in the *National Geographic*s, I would have been utterly shocked to discover how explicit these texts were. It's part and parcel of the invisible nature of adult female sexuality in our culture that it surprised me exactly zero that most dads had a stash of *Playboy*s somewhere that we could pilfer in order to get some sense of what would happen to us after puberty (*surprise! not that!*), but I didn't give a single thought to the moms packing their own porn fantasies in long, unillustrated tomes with embossed lettering on the covers. I definitely never gave much thought, either, to just how big a business romance novels were in the 1970s and '80s until I read a book by a feminist historian named Janice Radway called *Reading the Romance* (1984) that plunges the depths of the phenomenon that was the best-selling romance novel of the 1970s.

These novels were a second coming of the "trash" that Hawthorne dismissed. Part of their phenomenal success, Radway explains, was the development of a new kind of binding glue that allowed for the production of supercheap mass-market editions— the kind at the grocery store with Fabio or someone Fabio-like on the cover that we all know to mock so well. This mirrors the "paperback revolution" of the

1860s, when cheap editions by female writers really began to take off. Another similarity between the "scribbling women" and this era of the romance industry, unlike any other aspect of twentieth-century publishing, is that it incorporated readers in every step of the process of producing these fictions. Romance was not just a market; it was a subculture (or what the contemporary theorist Lauren Berlant has identified as a "counter-public"—a group of cultural producers and consumers with a for-us-by-us mentality).

Radway reveals that the very best-selling of these best-selling titles, the real game changers, were not produced by the professional writers or contract pens-for-hire who tried to jump on the lucrative bandwagon of appealing to this vast reading population. They were written by amateur women writers who had read scores and scores of romance novels before writing the one they had to write because it was the one they wished they could buy and read. In this way, romance is a genre not unlike the genre we think of as "literary fiction." A part of what marks a "serious" work of literary fiction is its own awareness of the literary fictions that preceded it—its ability to plug into and expand on a preexisting aesthetic tradition. It's the same with romance novels.

One can't write a great literary novel without first reading a lot of literary novels, nor can one write a great romance novel without first reading a lot of romance novels. One of the best known and most successful of the kind of romance writers who steeped herself in romance novels until she simply had to write the kind of book she wanted to read was Rosemary Rogers. A single mother with limited resources, Rogers sent the manuscript for a novel she called *Sweet Savage Love* unsolicited to an editor at Avon Books at the urging of her daughter. This work was unlike the others that came before it, in that the story's rough sex scenes formed a major part of the text: no fading out after the kissing here, folks. At the time, Rogers could have no way of knowing how much her unprecedented work would change her own life, the lives of millions of readers, or the entire industry that grew around the new developments in fiction geared toward women readers that it pioneered.

Like so many of the best-selling bodice-rippers that followed it, *Sweet Savage Love* is set in circumstances of political turmoil—both the American Civil War and the Mexican Liberal Reform. There's actually a huge amount of historical information and context in this very, very long novel. (A paperback copy runs to 712 pages.) The hero is a soldier in the Union army named Steve Morgan, which may be the most historically inaccurate thing about the whole work because I've never, in all of my reading in the nineteenth century, encountered a nineteenth-century guy named "Steve" rather than "Stephen," and this ruins it a bit in that Steve to me is like DJ Tanner's

dim-witted boyfriend in *Full House* or Maeby Fün-
ke's basic jock crush Steve Holt in *Arrested Development*—a lug whose greatest conquests take place in
front of a fridge.

Steve Morgan is the opposite of that. He speaks
countless languages; he's apparently the most skilled
marksman, knife fighter, wilderness survivor, con
man, hit man, lover, etc. to have ever lived. In the
beginning, his love affair with a young, sheltered
virgin from the American South, Ginny Brandon,
seems like a contemporary version of a classic
Reconstruction-era romance plot (novels written
following the American Civil War that dramatize the
reunification of the nation through a North-South
love story). But Steve Morgan is not just a Union
solider—that's more like a gig than a career for him.

Once Steve kidnaps Ginny, she comes with him
on a wild ride across the continent that reveals him
to be, at first, in league with the revolutionary Juaris-
tas and then, later, the son of the richest landowner
in Mexico and heir to a vast estate. The difference
between them is that Steve is the one doing all of
the raping and warring, while Ginny is the one trying to figure out how she feels about it. Steve spends
the novel killing people and stealing horses. Ginny
spends it pacing around bedrooms, obsessing over
Steve and waiting for him to return. The theorist
Andrea Long Chu defines as female "any psychic op-
eration in which the self is sacrificed to make room
for the desires of another," and Ginny's bedroom-

pacing is a pretty solid dramatization of the feminine psyche's fundamental other-focus. When she's pacing, Ginny is grappling with how her desires for Steve fit into her disapproval of the structure of their relationship and the greater structures of the world that relationship represents.

In a *Political Unconscious* mode of reading, this reveals to us that for women, sex is never just about sex. By depicting the actual sex, rather than doing the literary equivalent of a cinematic fade-out, Rogers gives readers something more than titillation. Bodice-ripper sex scenes—which are rarely if ever closely interpreted when these novels are written about—offer valuable insight into how the desire for rough sex with dangerous men functions and why it exists. Both Steve and Ginny use their sexual relationship as a way to work out their understanding of how they fit into the world, and their sexual relationship is charged by their constant grappling over power. Like Capitola, Ginny resents Steve's male privilege, but his exercise of it also arouses her. Like Black Donald, Steve resents how Ginny challenges him, but her challenging behavior also arouses him. The mutual erotic charge is connected to their revolutionary politics. What's a revolution but a jockeying for who gets to be the whipper and who the horse? (Pun intended.) If the horse-taming trope is an allegory for political revolution as well as sex, the sexy shelter/threat combo is a figure for the simultaneous desire to belong and to overthrow. Of course, both Ginny and Steve are completely incapable of talking about this. Here's what it looks like when they try:

"But you're a man. If not tonight, then there can be other nights. You're free to ride where you please, when you please. It's so frustrating to be a woman, to have to wait until someone accompanies you. Sometimes I feel that being a woman is worse than being a child—we have the intelligence and the feelings of adults, but we aren't permitted to show them."

"Was that why you couldn't sleep? Because you feel frustrated and restless?" They were both kneeling, staring into each other's face. Her fingers plucked nervously at her skirt until he put his hand over hers, stilling its movement. "I wish—it seems as though every time we meet we are either quarrelling or—or—can't we talk?"

"This isn't the time or the place for talking, and I'm in no mood to play the gentleman and flirt with you under the stars, Ginny Brandon," he said roughly. Before she could answer he had pulled her to her feet, holding both her hands.

What their desire for each other contains is another desire: to strip away the inequities of their sociopolitical circumstances. She doesn't want to be subjugated, he doesn't want to "play gentleman," and yet they're both still wedded to the social roles into which they've been inserted. The only place we see a reconciliation of these conflicting urges is when they're fucking, and so fucking becomes a place of political and emotional refuge. Right after this conversation about not being able to communicate verbally, they have sex for the first time, which is also Ginny's first time ever:

> Ginny forced herself by an effort of will to lie acquiescent under his hands. She had wanted this—with one part of her mind she realized dimly that perhaps she had wanted to lie with him just this way from the very beginning, when he had first seized her and kissed her so brutally. But none of her imaginings had ever been like this reality— "the thing that men and women do together" that she and her friends had discussed in whispers at the convent as something terrible and frightening but inevitable, had surely nothing to do with what was happening now!
>
> Gentle, still kissing her, he was easing her arms from around his neck, and again Ginny shivered as she felt her gown, her last defense, slip from her body. She had not thought that he'd want her completely naked, and it was only by closing her eyes tightly and gritting her teeth together that she could control her own instinctive shyness and the protests that welled up in her throat.
>
> At least, thank God, he seemed to know exactly what to do, exactly how to still her unspoken fears. For all his previous roughness and harsh-

ness, he was now only gentle with her, his hands patient with her shrinking flesh.

His own fully clad body half covering hers now, his leg thrown over her to keep her still, his hands resumed their exploring—his fingers brushing like fire against her skin.

She felt his mouth on her breasts, lips and tongue teasing her nipples until she groaned, a muted, strangely incoherent sound, and at the same time, taking her by surprise, his hands moved lower.

"Don't, love—don't cross your legs against me. Your body is so beautiful you've no need to be ashamed of it . . ."

He kissed her hair and eyes and face and the pulse that beat in the hollow of her throat and then her breasts again until she was flushed and shaking with a recurrence of the same wild and thoughtless emotions that had swept over her before when he had held her and kissed her the last time, up in the hills.

Suddenly his hands were between her thighs, stroking the soft inner skin very gently, moving upward—she gave an instinctive, incoherent cry as his fingers found her and he muffled it against his mouth.

"Be still, love—I'll be gentle—just be still now—"

He spoke to her as softly and coaxingly as if she were a mare to be tamed and gentled for her first mounting, and after a while she forgot who she was and who he was and gave in, letting his fingers have their way, her body writhing and straining upward against his, aching for something she couldn't yet understand or recognize until she found it at last; her arms going upward to hold him closer, closer, her body straining against his until she came floating, shuddering back to reality, her eyes flying open.

Here, she gets to have the shame and its release; she gets to be the horse and Steve, too. When Rogers writes that Ginny must be tamed like a mare, she's tapping into a centuries-long way of talking about sex without talking about it—"the thing that men and women do together." For a moment, Ginny can feel unashamed about feeling ashamed. She can experience physical pleasure without feeling guilty about it because the guilt is both acknowledged and exorcised through the fucking. Once the fucking is over, she's like Natalie Imbruglia: illusion never changes into something real. During the fucking, they are enacting the gendered power imbalance as farce. Almost all sub/dom sexual fantasies have this aura of sociopolitical catharsis, from boss/secretary to cop play to sexual "slavery."

The classic feminist complaint—which, when I was briefly an editor of romance novels myself, I was quick to lodge—about these texts is that they glorify sexual violence. This critique has a long history and includes the tradition of both antiporn feminism and the feminist backlash to Freudian psychoanalytic theory, especially the bits that suggest the locus of female desire is the female experience of lack because women who don't have penises are sad about the fact that they don't have penises. If you believe the male Freudians, women are obsessed with not having penises. And if you believe the psychoanalytic feminists, women don't care that much about actual penises at all. Romance novels have a very different take on all this.

Rogers, and the many bodice-ripper writers that followed her, have a veritable obsession with describing the spectacle of the male erection. Just as, in the transition from the sentimental novel to the bodice-ripper, horsewhipping becomes actual depicted sex, the whip becomes an actual depicted penis. We're all familiar with how the female naked body is much more frequently displayed in filmed sex scenes. (I bet you can count the number of blockbuster movies with male full-frontal on one hand, but you'll be counting for a very long time if you attempt to do the same with fully naked female bodies.) Far less remarked on is how the male genitalia gets more referred to in writing. You know that myth about how Inuit people have hundreds of words for snow? That's what romance novels are like for dick. Member, manhood, rod, staff, sword, shaft, mast, cock—so on and so forth. References to female genitalia are most often prepositional: inside her, beneath her, on top of her, through her. I can see how easy it is to conclude that this kind of language disempowers women, that this is body shame extended to nondepiction. But I think the body shame is very separate from this particular aspect of bodice-ripper sex. One comes to a bodice-ripper to read about the throbbing member, and that member is saying something very specific. Because the hard cock of the bodice-ripper is not really about the power of the male phallus. It's about female sexual power and male shame.

Consider the trope of the teenage boy who must hide his erection behind his school notebook—in these circumstances, the erect penis ceases to be the ultimate symbol of male potency and dominance; it is instead cast as the man's uncontrollable biological response to his female partner, the very sign of her power. And limited though it may be, it is power nonetheless. Before Steve Morgan has violent sex with Ginny (and their sex seems to get more violent as it goes), he has violent sex with her stepmother, Sonya. The guy is nothing if not thorough. It's the first sex scene in the novel, and it occurs when he seeks refuge from the rain in her cabin. The English writers are to blame for this trope—there are a lot of ponds to fall into and unexpectedly rainy days in England, which is fortunate for people who are attracted to each other in Victorian novels and English romcoms because they are often accidentally drenching themselves to the near point of saying, "Let's get you out of those wet clothes." If you need a visual on this, see Colin Firth as Darcy emerging from the pond in the 1995 BBC television adaptation of *Pride and Prejudice*. It's not an actual scene in the actual Jane Austen novel, but it very well might and should be.

Anyhow, when Steve encounters Sonya in the cabin, basically the first thing she notices about him is his erection:

> His wet uniform, plastered closely to his body, left nothing to her imagination, not even the fact that he had begun to desire her. Instinctively, shockingly, Sonya's eyes had dropped downward, and now she raised them quickly with a muffled, horrified cry, her pale cheeks flushing bright crimson.
>
> "Do you expect me to apologize? There are some things a man cannot control, I'm afraid."

Because the dark hero represents the circumstances of oppression that the heroine seeks relief from in the form of sexual release, his erection becomes the one sign of "things a man cannot control" and, therefore, her control over him. Just as often as the heroine doesn't offer her consent in their initial encounters, so too does the hero become powerless over what the sight of her body does to his body. As the genre evolves, the erections are still front and center, but they even more explicitly signal female control. Consider this passage in the 2010 novel *Rose* by Jill Marie Landis:

Kase let her kiss him, but he steeled himself against the inevitable reaction. He kept his hands clamped around the edge of the chair seat, afraid to touch her, afraid of crushing her to him, of pouring out words of love. When she did not end the kiss, but demanded more of him—deepened the pressure on his lips and played her tongue against the seam of his mouth—Kase felt his body come alive with sensations he had denied himself for far too long. The blood pulsed in his veins and surged into his loins with every heartbeat as his desire and need for Rose heightened. He fought against his overwhelming need. . . . He groaned, half in protest, half in pleasure, when he felt her fingers loosen his waistband and then move down to free the buttons along the front of his pants. His throbbing member came to attention upon release.

A part of the fantasy of social upheaval here is the giant, dark, powerful man made powerless in the face of his overwhelming desire—the tyrant reduced to a throbbing member. What Kase is so reluctant to give in to here, it's worth noting, is "pouring out words of love." Rose eventually gains the acceptance she craves through the power of her sexuality.

In these throbbing-member scenes, sex is like a contest in which the one who wants it more loses. It's a no-brainer to understand, given everything I've already said, why, from a cultural perspective, women might want to pretend not to want it. But if male sexual power is defined by social, political, and physical dominance, the proof of this power is not a man's using his dominance to take a woman by force but, rather, when his performance of dominance is so convincing that she succumbs to him willingly. Since it's dominance she wants, if he has to really *force* her, his dominance is unconvincing. These sex scenes may start out forcefully, but as Ginny "let[s] his fingers have their way, her body writhing and straining upward against his, aching for something she couldn't yet understand or recognize until she found it at last," the female participant always gets into it. Even if the hero doesn't necessarily know that, the readers do.

It's the nature of desire—and not violence—that both parties want the other person to want it more than they do. After hundreds of years of bonnet-wearing and needlepoint, not to mention a different kind of anatomical setup, women are much better at hiding their physical desire. So while the world is almost always a more winning proposition for the hero of the bodice-ripper—paradoxically, even when she is being "carried off," to use Capitola's euphemism—the bedroom is a more winning proposition for the heroine.

This may be troubling to say the least, largely because a central conceit of rape culture is that men can't control their own desire. Women in conservative cultures are made to cover their bodies for the sake of men. "Asking for it" is the justificatory trope of rapists and their defenders—as if the possession of a female body is enough to make one responsible for its violation. But the rough sex in romance novels is different not only because real rape is about a desire for violence rather than a desire for sex but also because bodice-ripper sex is depicted in a safe space of female fantasy. The novel for women and by women taps into a kind of power that women *do* wield that, like our bodies themselves, we've been taught to feel ashamed of.

Male critics like René Girard have become highly respected intellectuals by describing a similar process to what I see at work in the bodice-ripper but in the context of male literature and male issues. Girard explains that the male hero of fiction is almost always experiencing some form of what he calls *askesis*. This is a Greek word with the same root as "ascetic"—the person who practices severe self-discipline and denial, like Beyoncé on a juice cleanse. The hero must deny himself something, whether that be spiritual fulfillment, social acceptance, or the kind of sex he wants to have. Describing how this *askesis* works to create conflict, Girard writes, "Consciousness loses control over the process. Resistance to desire becomes increasingly painful but it no longer depends on a voluntary decision. Torn by two forces pulling in opposite directions, the subject becomes prey to fascination. Originally he refused to yield to desire for tactical reasons; now he finds he is incapable of such a surrender." Girard identifies two opposing themes that make this *askesis* thing so powerful: the total self-control of the "Don-Juan protagonist" and what he calls the "Stendhalian Fiasco"—the hero's physical impotence in the face of extreme desire. I'm very on board with Girard when he suggests, referencing perhaps the malest book ever written, *The Sun Also Rises* (1926), "Ernest Hemingway's work would be more truthful if Jake, instead of being a war cripple, simply presented the other side of those marvelously flegmatic [*sic*] beings whose superb virility we admire in the other novels." What he means is that Jake's inability to get it up is merely the other side of the coin of the "virile" hero's inability to keep it down. The opposite of the throbbing member is not the war-injured penis but the fantasy of perfect male control.

If sex becomes a competition about who wants it less, one romantic fantasy solves both parties' problems almost perfectly, and therefore it's no surprise it's a pretty common one. We might think of it as the "Sleeping Beauty"—a plot in which everyone manipulated by the heteropatriarchy momentarily wins. Most fairy tales are vaguely about rape (Little Red Riding Hood and the wolf, Goldilocks and the bears, the girl in Rumpelstiltskin forced to spin, etc.), but no plot so completely and clearly conjures it in the same way as "Sleeping Beauty." That chick is just a pretty girl lying unconscious, waiting for someone to kiss her. She can't consent because she's asleep. What this circumstance does for her is prevent her from having to admit that she has any sexual desire at all, because women get desire shame just as badly as men do—more badly in fact, because the proposition of her own sexual desire arouses not just a humiliating loss of control but also that old shame about unchasteness. In *Sweet Savage Love*, Sonya admits as much to Steve Morgan, after he reveals he's powerless to control his erection, and then they end up fucking *again*:

> "Oh, God, I'm so ashamed!" she whispered brokenly, and felt him kiss her tear-wet cheek again, and then her mouth. Gradually, her body warmed and stirred under his roving hands, and she began to murmur incoherently and clutch at his shoulders; her head shaking in silent protest even while her body moved to accept him once more.

Their sex is the quintessential battle over who can more successfully avoid their desire. And it's pleasurable sex because it involves both the body and the brace—the mutual desire and the mutual shame at gratifying it. Just as sex is a bond, shame is a bond. Hence the hotness of affairs and secret trysts and the Sharks and the Jets and *Romeo and Juliet* and so on and so forth. So, in the Sleeping Beauty plot, if she gets to be released from this double bind by being asleep, he gets to be released from it by being unseen. As Girard writes, "Desire can be released from the [desirer] only if the beloved, for some reason or other, is unable to see her lover and feel his caresses. This lover need no longer fear that he may reveal to his beloved the humiliating spectacle of his own desire." The fact that Sleeping Beauty is asleep also ensures that she won't see her prince, so his erection never becomes a "humiliating spectacle."

When Girard says "for some reason or other," he's right again. There are many plot scenarios that allow for this release from the *askesis* problem, and they have produced an enduring series of tropes I see in women's fictions from at least the nineteenth century to the present. The reason these issues have been less considered in women's fiction is not only that women's fictions are, on the whole, taken less seriously and are therefore less frequently fodder for more theoretical critical work but also that feminist critics have been more reluctant to see these plots as liberatory for women, as they employ the very tropes of rape culture we've long understood to be oppressive. Yet the acknowledgment and even ownership of these oppressive tropes is central to our ability to access pleasure. And we must also acknowledge that the pleasure of oppressed people is a liberatory end in itself. A significant part of that pleasure, too, is bearing witness to the very fact of oppression—political oppression as well as the oppressive nature of desire itself.

In Greek myth, Eros wears a blindfold. Traditionally, this is because "love is blind": you can't control whom you want. But it's also because, I think along with Girard, it's humiliating to acknowledge your own desire. Desire implies an incompleteness: we desire what we do not have. Desire implies a lack of power: if you know what someone wants, they're more easily controlled. Seeing the thing or person I desire can make me, to quote the twentieth-century R&B artists/theorists Sisters With Voices, "so weak in the knees I can hardly speak. I lose all control and something takes over me." It's much easier to experience this barrage of disempowerment without looking right at the object of desire or, worse yet, being looked at by them.

This is why the erotics of domination so often include masks. I will not stop to get to the bottom of the mystery that is the masked ball in the Selena Gomez masterpiece *Another Cinderella Story* (2008), where no one can seem to recognize who anyone is despite the fact that everyone is wearing only very minimal masks that cover half of their faces, nor will I ask the same of *The Princess Bride*'s Wesley's apparently shocking reappearance as the Dread Pirate Roberts. I will only briefly mention (like, this is it) Zorro, Batman, the Lone Ranger, and the very disturbing internet search I conducted using the term "sexy masked men." (Not recommended but obviously you're doing it anyway.)

Our old friend Black Donald is constantly in disguises as a part of his villainous plots. At one point, he dresses as "an elderly field preacher," fooling everyone in town. How are you going to believe Jason Momoa in that role? When a person is six feet eight in 1859, can he really be anyone but himself? Because this part of the plot so intrepidly tests our suspension of disbelief, you know it has to be important. When Black Donald is disguised, he can see everyone else, but no one else can see the real him. Disguises and hidden identities are all over Disney sexuality as well. Cinderella turns out to be the rushed hottie at the ball; Prince Charming is that stranger encountered in the woods; Prince Ali and the mysterious street urchin Aladdin are one and the same; Mulan, the truculent soldier, is actually a girl whom Captain Li Shang can get down with heterosexually. It's how the lovers get what they want without having to admit they want it. The disguise is the guilt. It is the mask and the face, the body and the brace. The bodice-ripper isn't hot without acknowledging there's a bodice to be ripped off in the first place. Saying "it's just a guilty pleasure" is drawing a circle of guilt around the experience of guilty media consumption. The phrase itself is a mask.

* * *

Reading or watching these stories offers us all of the pleasure without the guilt excised. It's such an effective means of catharsis that we get it again and again, in similar plots repeated. To say that romance novels "aren't good" because they're the same thing over and over is not only a blunt comment about genre (there are, really, many different plots going) but also a blunt comment about sex and indeed the experience of everyday life itself. And so we put on our bras and our lipstick. We shave our legs and pluck our brows and dye our gray hairs brown and blond and red. We worry about our shirt buttons becoming undone at the chalkboard, our breasts accidentally becoming part of a collegial hug. We carry our keys in our hands through the dark parking lot and check the locks on all the doors before going to bed. In the course of my own life, these diurnal rhythms have been a constant. "Let's walk another way," my female colleague says casually as we approach a darkened corridor between buildings in broad daylight, and I agree to shift our path without saying a word about it, continuing our professional conversation. I know why. She needn't explain. It is the everydayness of these practices that wears one down, far more than the monolith of their political and cultural significance. While we may wish for them to change, fight for them to change, they do not change; so another part of why the romance is cathartic and pleasurable is because the romance doesn't attempt to change things in a durable way.

Unlike explicitly feminist texts or political scholarship that purport to encourage a call to action (but are actually, themselves, engaged in a cycle of repetition—repeatedly calling for the same changes that never occur), romances demand nothing of their readers beyond their own experience of pleasure. They do not force us to do hard work, to labor for our own liberation, or even our own survival, every single day while we endure the lack of power we have over it. They create a moment of not doing the work and not even pretending to care about it—a spiritual rest we all deserve.

When Ginny and Steve aren't fucking in *Sweet Savage Love,* they're back to the old circumstances of social domination. She's pacing the bedroom while the readers are cleaning the toilet, picking the kids up from school, being harassed on the street for being too hot or not hot enough. As the critic Saidiya Hartman writes in her article "The End of White Supremacy, An American Romance," about a speculative romance story by W. E. B. Du Bois called "The Comet," which imagines an interracial romance during the apocalypse as a fantasy of racial reconciliation,

> It won't defeat the world or make them immortal or shield them from gratuitous violence, or spare the children, but they are grateful for love. Of all the things that love makes possible: eyes that see you, someone to hold your hand until the end, adore you even in your ugliness, kiss you a thousand times, hold you when you are carrying on like that bitch, do everything for your baby, even swing a knife for your love, risk it all for one last dance, exchange vows even when there isn't a chance in hell of being together, see heaven all in her eyes, carry a corpse-child through the devastated city in search of him, miss her until it breaks you, not want anybody else to ever love you, the one thing it is not able to do is confer a legacy

or guarantee a future. Your love is all I need—a beautiful lie, a necessary refrain that helps you survive in the meantime, experience tragedy after tragedy, endure another scene of grief, as if "our love" was fortification and always enough.

It helps you survive in the meantime. For people who live with their own oppression, it is always the meantime—and the meantime is very long. The real and important desire to overthrow the circumstances of one's own oppression does not contain within it a solution for the meantime. In the meantime, we must find ways to experience pleasure amid the circumstances of shame and violence that form our daily lives. And that's important, too.

2

EXPENSIVE SHEETS

Complex personhood means that even those
called "other" are never that. Complex personhood means that the stories people tell about
themselves, about their troubles, about their
social worlds, and about their society's problems are entangled and weave between what is
immediately available as a story and what their
imaginations are reaching towards. . . . Complex
personhood means that even those who haunt
our dominant institutions and their systems of
value are haunted too by things they sometimes
have names for and sometimes do not.

—Avery Gordon

There's a scene in Issa Rae's HBO comedy series *Insecure* in which the main character (played by Rae, also
named Issa) heads to her neighbor Eddie's apartment
with designs on a casual hookup. When she arrives,
he's intently watching *Gossip Girl*.

> "Blake Lively's doin' her thing," Eddie says.
>   "Is that the white girl?" asks Issa before adding,
> "I guess they're all white."

"They're white people," Eddie agrees.

"There's so many of them."

He nods. "It's good to see them doin' their thing."

Eddie's love of *Gossip Girl* seems to be an indicator that Issa shouldn't be there trying to get with him, and this is made far clearer when she leans in to kiss him and only succeeds in painfully bashing their faces together. Eddie is Issa's bottom-of-the-barrel hookup, the guy she seeks to get with when she's feeling the lowest, the one she thinks is safe because he's so far beneath her that he'd never reject her. She clearly doesn't get why Eddie likes watching *Gossip Girl*, but unlike Issa and her best friend, Molly, the show's other protagonist, we only ever see Eddie interacting with white people through the TV. He likes to see them "doin' their thing" on the Upper East Side from his couch in Inglewood.

Insecure seems unique among streaming shows in that its characters spend a lot of time watching TV. This theme was a staple of nineties sitcoms like *Married with Children* and *The Simpsons*, but in *Insecure* we get to spend more time with what they're watching—some of it real programming like *Gossip Girl* and some of it fictional programming specifically filmed for the show-within-a-show—and more time watching them discuss what they're watching with each other. One made-up program Issa and her friends love is called *Due North*. It's a melodrama set in the antebellum South that follows the love triangle between two African American slaves and their white master. How to get free is *Due North*'s main dilemma, but how to curry the romantic interest of the master is the entertaining plotline that dominates the clips of the show that *Insecure* viewers get to see, featuring lines like "You let Massa swing low on your sweet chariot?!" that garner laughs from both the characters on *Insecure* and the real-life audience watching them watch.

Just as bodice-rippers offer a cathartic answer to the problem of the gender revolution that never seems to come, *Due North* is a place where the characters in *Insecure* congregate to release the unremitting pressures of being a Black woman in America. *Due North* is presented as their guilty pleasure just as *Gossip Girl* is Eddie's. But why is he watching it? *Gossip Girl* is an excellent example of a genre I call *rich white people fictions* (henceforward RWPFs)— books, movies, and shows about very rich and very white people. RWPFs offer a fantasy of the power that superwealth and superwhiteness confer. They're a form of escapism akin to superhero movies: they indulge us by imagining what it would be like to move through the world effortlessly, to inhabit an experience so elevated from the experience of everyone else. To take pleasure in imagining this kind of power translates to a real desire no more so than watching a Marvel movie would make you want to quit your day job for a full-time career in crime-fighting and Spandex—and no more than enjoying a bodice-ripper translates into a real desire for sexual violence. In order to understand effortlessness as a fantasy, which it most certainly is, we need only to look at the very small numbers of people who might see themselves in the depictions of RWP, as compared to the millions who enthusiastically consume these fictions—a great many of whom are neither rich nor white in any sense.

It's a pleasure, in this world of abject suffering, to watch the RWP fictionally not suffering. I, for instance, take comfort in a Jane Austen heroine on a long walk, because the walk highlights the absolutely vast stretches of free time that she has and that I do not. I am reliably pleased by the phrase "I'll call you a car" or, better yet, "[chauffer's name] will take you." I like when the hunting party returns to Downton and the servants are there waiting for them outside the house with wine in silver goblets. Even in darker, more self-aware fare like *The Crown* or *Succession*, these RWP always come out on top. In these fictions, RWP are especially winning in matters of love, because, given their complete material comfort, certainly they merit, RWPFs imply, emotional satisfaction too. And I root for them! They are like teammates in a sport I love but am not good at. And when they win it all for the team, inside of me I am cheering my face off. It's not my victory. But I was there.

By thinking about how whiteness is disrupted, even within fictions wherein it might appear that *all* of the characters are white, I've come to see how RWPFs cater to the guilty pleasures of domination. It happens here on a slightly different axis than bodice-rippers or Judy Blume books, but RWPFs nevertheless offer a similar catharsis by granting viewers access to the experience of economic and racial power while simultaneously acknowledging it will never be theirs to have.

When I start to think about whiteness—especially the whiteness of fictional characters—as a structure of power rather than a physical trait, who is and who is not considered white undergoes relational shifts. In some circumstances, an individual may be the whiter person; in others, their power is diminished by another person's superior claims to whiteness. To me, the subject of RWPFs is always whiteness and its fictionality. I think that when we accept whiteness as a central theme of popular fictions, we can stop seeing it as a neutral category, an absence of race rather than what it is—the enforcement of the hierarchical idea of race. Truth be told, though as a concept it's probably created more devastation than any other concept going, I think all whiteness is pretty fictional.

W. E. B. Du Bois famously wrote about the phenomenon of "double-consciousness" that black people in America experience: "It is a peculiar sensation, this double-consciousness, this sense of always looking at one's self through the eyes of others, of measuring one's soul by the tape of a world that looks on in amused contempt and pity." What is double-consciousness but a form of mandatory other-focus? Though not identical, we see Du Bois's legacy in Andrea Long Chu's formulation of femaleness as a subordination of one's own desires to that of another and, furthermore, her observation that "the truth is, you are not the central transit hub for meaning about yourself. . . . You do not get to consent to yourself, even if you might deserve the chance." In the RWPFs I discuss here, the race and class identities of the non-RWP characters get formed through their interactions with RWP. Race and class cease to work as monoliths and become instead a series of things that happen to certain characters, shaping their understandings of themselves through external forces.

I like James Baldwin's formulation for white people, which is "the people who think of themselves as white." That way of putting it taps into the magisterial claims of whiteness, its grand delusion. The delusional claim to whiteness has been as successful as it has been destructive and genocidal. Here I'm going to think less about the violent political wages of whiteness and wealth inequity and more about the guilty pleasures these structures of power afford the imaginary. In a nation where, increasingly, fewer and fewer people are rich and white, why are shows and movies about rich white people still so beloved? What's happening when average, systematically disenfranchised Americans gather around their televisions to warm themselves by the glow of *Downton Abbey*, *Revenge*, *Big Little Lies*, or *Sex and the City*?

A bizarrely literal illustration of how the fantastical powers of fictional rich whiteness work is to be found in the 2013 British romantic comedy *About Time*, written and directed by Richard Curtis, screenwriter of such British RWPFs as *Notting Hill* (1999) and *Four Weddings and a Funeral* (1994). *About Time* is, like many RWPFs, also a romcom, and it centers on Tim Lake, a member of the English landed gentry who grows up in a rambling waterfront country estate in Cornwall with his delightfully eccentric RWP family. (They take tea on the lawn! They wear those silly paper crowns at Christmas!) The unique twist in this movie about a wealthy white guy looking for love is that Tim Lake also has a literal superpower. As his father tells him one winter night, "The secret is that the men in the family can travel in time."

What seems like a parody of the power of rich whiteness is actually true here. Tim finds that if he makes an awkward comment or a bad decision, he can step into a dark space, close his eyes, and will himself to go back in time—fifteen minutes, an hour, a year—in order to right his ship. It's a delicious fantasy of power, the ultimate solution to having said or done the wrong thing. *If only I had another chance*, I so often think in the wake of my own many missteps and humiliations, *I could do it right this time*.

Two things interest me about this superpower: first, only the men in this fabulously wealthy, very

English, very white family have it; and second, although its presence in the movie seems to mark a generic shift to the supernatural, *About Time* is still pretty much a realistic romcom. That's because the "superpower" is only a slight acceleration of the power the men in Tim's family already wield. Their ability to time-travel is just one part of the fantasy of their social dominance that includes living in a gorgeous beach house or, as Tim also does, moving to a friend of the family's London townhouse to take up a career in law that is easily gotten through family connections. (What a delight compared to, say, calculating algorithms about the relationship between how long it will take me to find a job and how long it is socially acceptable to sleep on my friend's couch.) How smooth life is for the RWP! Being one is a superpower unto itself. Just think of the ease with which fictional male RWP get to make things happen—it's Christian Gray whisking Annabelle away in a helicopter, Richard Gere buying Julia Roberts all of the jewelry and clothes her heart desires, *The Prince and Me*, *Maid in Manhattan*, *Ever After*, even *Crazy Rich Asians*—wherein the Chinese, not the mostly unportrayed, darker-skinned South Asians that make up the majority of Singapore's working classes, have the structural power of whiteness. This effortless power is the fundamental fantasy of the RWPF. Part of the pleasure of watching is dwelling in the structures of inequity that make the protagonists so rich and so white.

In RWPFs, seemingly everything is white: the sheets, the furniture, the kitchen countertops. There are so many tennis whites, brunch whites, white napkins and tablecloths. There are the aspirationally crisp white shirts of Diane Keaton, a feminized version of Jay Gatsby's wrinkle-free white linen suit. There was the entire personality of Tom Wolfe. Toni Morrison persuasively argues in her 1992 book *Playing in the Dark* that images of whiteness (white objects, white spaces) are conjured in literature to imply the subordination of Africanness. There is no whiteness without nonwhiteness, no colonizer in white linen sipping his gin and tonic without the darker peoples doing the laundry and slicing the limes. These white objects of fiction are the physical manifestations of the hitchlessness of the rich, white experience. Non-RWP cannot wear all white in everyday life without stains and smudges, spills and rips. Non-RWP wear black so the splashes of oil and patches of sweat don't show. They design their kitchens to hide the dirt and the dents. The RWPF fantasy is the possibility of release from all of that.

* * *

But escapism is not all the RWPFs offer. There's also a much deeper payoff. I think a large part of the appeal of RWPFs for femme subjects is that they explain to us why most of us have not had access to the amount and kind of love we crave. The reason this fantasy is so compelling is because it's partially true. Though not a guarantee of all the love and happiness I desire, my life would be easier if I were richer and whiter. That's how the game is rigged. Acknowledging that in a backhanded way lets me off the hook. This is precisely the fantasy behind *Home Again*, a 2017 film made by Hallie Meyers, daughter of Nancy Meyers (queen director of RWPFs known for their particularly white, gorgeous kitchens). Reese Witherspoon plays Alice, a middle-aged mom separated from a husband who's grown bored of her. Now that's an everywoman story right there. But there are a couple of twists that make it less so: one is that Alice looks like Reese Witherspoon. Another is that her father was a famous film auteur with a drop-dead-gorgeous (white, of course) family home in LA that is hers for the taking when she decides to leave New York after her marriage sours. (This is a real house that Ben Affleck and Jennifer Garner lived in until they sold it in 2009 for $6.25 million.)

Because of these twists, what happens next seems precisely as likely for most viewers as owning a $6.25 million home, which is that three attractive men in their twenties whom Alice meets in a bar come to live in her guesthouse and all fall madly in love with her—though she only ends up having deep, soul-satisfying sex with one of them because she is a woman of principle. I, for one, can easily enjoy the fantasy of a gorgeous, ambitious, and sensitive man in the prime of his youth wanting nothing more than to indulge his voracious appetite for a single mom in her forties because I know that the reason it's off-limits to me is that I do not in any way resemble Reese Witherspoon and I am by no means super crazy rich. The film is not subtle about this. It is quite direct about the fact that this is why they're all in love with her. The morning after their first night in the home, the young visitors discover evidence that this is the famous filmmaker's house and that Alice is his daughter. As if this isn't enough, Alice's mother (played by RWP Candice Bergen), who starred in his films, comes by. "I can't believe you're here. And you're you. This is surreal," one of the young men tells her. These young men are what I call the "poor test characters" of an RWPF: there to bear witness to the superior richness and whiteness of the protagonists. Just like the viewer on her IKEA couch in leggings she bought at Marshall's (me), these young, Semitic men have become aware that they've stepped into an RWPF.

So much of *Home Again* is built around the darker, poorer young men's expressions of devotion to both the achievement of a dream that Alice's rich, white father represents (they're aspiring filmmakers) and the fantastic possessions that his success has enabled Alice to enjoy. Once established in Alice's guest-house, they marvel at the quality of her sheets. One of the guys, George, says to the others, "You've gotta feel these sheets. Oh, wow, these sheets are insane! What are they made of?" He could be voicing a review of the entire movie. And I never tire of it. Just as early twentieth-century readers of Edith Wharton's novels loved the details upon details that she piled on to lengthy descriptions of her characters' clothes and interiors and *Sex and the City* fans meticulously blogged every outfit its characters wore, RWPF viewers are here for the sheets. I, for one, want to express wonder at not even knowing what they could possibly be made of. Angel feathers? Babies' skin? No real sheets could ever be as soft as these fictional sheets—just as no one can be quite as rich and as white as Alice.

Without Alice's extraordinary white wealth, the plot of *Home Again* would be utterly inexplicable. Far worse, it would imply that the average viewer could have this happen: three younger men fighting over her at the exact moment her previously unappreciative husband returns to win her back. It's just wonderful to see how much chaos everyone's ardent love for her creates. When Alice's husband returns to find this trio of hunks sniffing around his estranged wife, his conversation with them ends up in fisticuffs in Alice's impossibly long and well-landscaped driveway. No one's fighting in the driveway over me, but that's not my fault. My sheets are like two-hundred-thread-count cotton at best.

Americans in particular cherish the fantasy that we are just one new, more elevated consumption style away from love and fulfillment. It's why we engage in guilty pleasures beyond fictions, too. *Just this new top, this new hair color, this new juicer will make all the difference.* If I can't buy the house with the guesthouse and the pool house and the carriage house, I can buy a throw pillow that might belong there, and though it won't grant me such fantastic rewards, maybe it will make me more real, more like the kind of woman who is showered with love.

Both whiteness and richness in these fictions have no horizon. No matter how white and how rich a character may seem, it's always possible that someone else is richer and whiter and therefore more deserving of love. In the 1991 remake of *Father of the Bride*, the endless possibilities of rich whiteness pleasurably stimulate the desire to be loved the way the bride in that movie is by her father (Steve Martin), by her mother (Diane Keaton), and even by her little brother (Kieran Culkin, Macaulay's brother), for gods' sakes. "I love you, Annie," the little Culkin croons to her so sweetly from across the hall after she says good night. So beloved are these rich white Alices and Annies! So coddled and so dear.

The suburban California house that this family lives in looks a lot like the Illinois house of the bigger Culkin from *Home Alone*, released the previous year. In both films, the house and the rich white Americanness it suggests—both houses are also, of course, white (their "impenetrable whiteness," to use Morrison's term, is what these films are all about)—is a major establishing point. Steve Martin's character, George, tells us in voice-over, "I love this house. I love that I taught my kids to ride their bikes in the driveway. I love that I slept with them in tents in the backyard. I love that we carved our initials in the tree out front. This house is warm in the winter, cool in the summer, and looks spectacular with Christmas lights. It's a great house." His love for his family is all bound up in his love for the big, white house. And it *is* absolutely stunning. It's also a real house, where they shot many of the outside scenes, in Alhambra, California. In 2016, it sold for $2 million. George Banks can easily afford such a property. We learn shortly after his paean to the house that he also owns an entire factory that daily fills with people who work for him making sneakers. At this early point, I'm utterly convinced he could not possibly wish to be any richer. What is the factory owner if not a monopoly-man trope of white wealth?—for example, Veruca Salt's dad in *Charlie and the Chocolate Factory* (1971). But here the unthinkable happens to that trope: George and Nina (Diane Keaton) are humbled by the MacKenzies, the exponentially richer parents of the guy their daughter met on a study-abroad semester in Italy.

"Where is your bathroom?" George asks Mr. and Mrs. MacKenzie on his first visit to their Bel Air mansion.

"It's the seventh door on the left."

"The second?"

"The *seventh*."

This exchange is supposed to be a joke. What's absolutely bananas about this RWPF iteration is that George Banks, the guy who initially presents as the rich white dad of escapist dreams, is suddenly remade into the poor test character, shamed for his simple tastes like backyard barbecues and top-of-the-line espresso machines—that's his wedding gift to his daughter, while the MacKenzies buy the couple a brand-new red convertible! The rest of the movie is actually, unbelievably, about George's financial insecurity. Every aspect of the wedding-planning process sends him into apoplectic fits about how much money he'll be forced to spend on his little girl's big day—money he can't refuse to spend because it will shame him in the eyes of the even richer RWP that are his in-laws.

But, you see, George Banks is going insane over this wedding because he really, really, really loves his daughter. This is the aspect of the film that, against all odds, makes it so heartwarming. In a movie where the richer-than-rich dad's communications with his Latina maid in broken Spanish seem to be positioned as some kind of perverse virtue signaling (a man of the people!), it's still incredibly moving to see regular-rich George play basketball in the drive-way with his daughter the night before her wedding. When it begins to snow and she stops midlayup to ask him what he's thinking, he says, "I'm thinking I'll remember this moment for the rest of my life." I can't be sure about you, but I just about die right there on the spot every time.

There's something so femme about wanting something really, really badly and enjoying its depiction more because it's delivered within a context entirely removed from the reality of my own life. How much sexier, sure, but also how much safer to read about a dangerous affair with an eighteenth-century Scottish Highlander than with a mildly good-looking guy from a workplace not dissimilar to my own. The safety comes not from avoiding the desire for things I might actually try to get but from avoiding truly wanting things I know I'll almost certainly never have. Who among us has parents even remotely like Steve Martin and Diane Keaton, who indulge in rapturous fantasies about every single time we slid effortlessly down a colonial bannister atop a shining row of hand-carved spindles? Indeed, who can even effortlessly slide down a bannister? (If I had tried to do this, my parents would have surely scolded me for jeopardizing the structural integrity of the staircase and potentially causing an expensive trip to the ER.) A pleasure to be had by RWPFs is, in a way, that the escapism is only partial. I can't completely lose myself in it. These fictions simultaneously allow for me to indulge in a fantasy of another kind of life while all the time dropping reminders that this is a very rarefied circumstance to which I, like the vast majority of viewers, will never have access. So it is not my fault if I am not loved in the way its characters are.

Even the seemingly whitest and richest of characters have a fundamental flaw that reminds us of the general unobtainability of rich whiteness. One of George Banks's many wedding faux pas is that, in an attempt to save on a tuxedo, he buys one off a friend who deals in black-market goods. The friend assures him it's a real Armani, but the truth comes out only when he dons it on his daughter's wedding day to find that it's navy—a color Armani apparently did not offer. The movie positions this slipup as the most humiliating imaginable thing. (I actually like the idea of a navy tuxedo, but maybe I wouldn't have in 1991? I don't think I spent any time considering tuxedos then, so hard to say.) Nevertheless, the blue tuxedo is like the wrong bonnet: a perfect metaphor for George's situation. George is the navy to the MacKenzies' black—just a shade off that he himself can't see unless it's placed right next to something truly black. If it's such a subtle difference of shade, if it's that hard to tell anyway, does it really matter? The RWP answer is emphatically *yes, it matters more than anything else in this oyster that is our world*. That's why so many RWP of fiction are plagued by fake luxuries. There is, for example, *Frasier*, season 1, episode 6, when the whiter-than-white radio psychiatrist (here's a fun game: what's a whiter name, Kelsey Grammar or Frasier Crane?) throws a cocktail party to celebrate the purchase of a new painting (really), only to discover it's a fake—for shame! Or the season 3 episode of *Sex and the City*, "Sex and Another City," in which Samantha buys a fake Fendi bag, only to have it stolen, which the women collectively agree is a well-deserved "karmic" punishment for buying imitation designer goods.

Such plots encourage viewers to engage in that same process—turn themselves inside out and check their proverbial seams and signatures, wondering if they are real. They also tip me off to the very fictiveness of whiteness itself: if even the people who seem to be the whitest have their doubts, maybe the very concept of whiteness requires such a profound suspension of disbelief that no real, experienced life can seem to fit inside it. The impenetrability of the RWP-world conjures my own inadequacy, their implausibility my own frustrations—because these fictions, despite their over-the-top premises, have a magical trick of making their world seem temporarily like the normal one and our own like the fake.

At the Banks's house, the water glasses on the table are crystal every night, as the film convincingly suggests they ought to be. The everydayness of the Banks's wealth is presented as practically hygienic. "They probably live in a shack," George speculates of his prospective in-laws before he meets them, as if this would close the case on their suspected moral failings. Does this fictional logic lead to the conclusion that if I didn't grow up in an eight-thousand-square-foot house shrouded in luxuriant bougainvillea, then I'm not worthy of love? Absolutely not. That's not the fantasy here. The fantasy is that if I *had* grown up in that house, the love I crave would have easily been mine. It releases me from thinking that it's my fault my dad never stopped to admire the way snowflakes glisten in my hair or that my fiancé never made a passionate speech to my parents about his love for me, practically screaming "I love your daughter!" after going on and on about how he wants to raise children and grandchildren with me and support my dreams because I'm the best goddamned architect to have ever lived.

The message I receive here is that if only everyone involved in my life had been whiter and richer, I'd be the talented architect whom everyone loves so much that it drives them insane. Rich whiteness is just out of reach—a mirage in the desert of despair where the hordes of parched wanderers can imagine some lucky individuals are enjoying a cool drink. *Father of the Bride* is set on the banks of that pool that will forever exist in a liminal space between fiction and reality; its covert message is, *You see? It has nothing to do with you.* And at that moment, the pleasure the film gives is its ability to release its viewers from their guilt. When I am enthralled by an RWPF, through every "if only" it poses, whatever sadness I have about the current state of my life becomes not my fault. I cannot go back in time to right my ship like Tim Lake, but my consolation is that my ship was never that seaworthy to begin with. I didn't know I was wearing the wrong tuxedo, and suddenly now I do; and that explains all the weird looks I've been getting for my entire life.

* * *

The next best thing in an RWPF to being an RWP is being around them (loving them, marrying into their families, sleeping in their sheets). To gain access to these privileges, one usually must be very hot. *Gossip Girl*'s Dan Humphreys (a poor test character if there ever was one) lives in a beautiful Williamsburg loft with very cool doors and attends a fancy private school but is impoverished by comparison to the Serena Van der Woodsens and Blair Waldorfs of the show. He only becomes a major player in the RWP social scene because his hotness is recognized. Same story for Julia Roberts in *Pretty Woman*, an obvious point given that the movie is actually just called that. RWP fictions like *Pretty Woman*, wherein the test character is allowed to enter the RWP world through sexual love, frequently feature a makeover scene. The person receiving the makeover is always hot to begin with. The object of the makeover is not an elevation of their physical beauty but an eradication of the poverty signaling of their previous look that reads to us as elevated hotness because it reads to us as elevated power. See *My Fair Lady*, *Can't Buy Me Love*, *The Prince and Me*, etc.

Hotness and its acquisition is another category of power that speaks to the fantasy of being able to move through the world without the friction of structural disadvantage. *About Time* is frothy and light, but it addresses very similar themes to the

1891 gothic novel *The Picture of Dorian Gray*, written by femme author extraordinaire Oscar Wilde, which is also about an RWP who uses a superpower to get whatever he wants. To my mind, the only way to understand this novel is as a detailed depiction of how rich whiteness works. Dorian's superpower is another kind of time-travel—a portrait that takes on all of the signs of his physical aging as well as his guilt. He does whatever he wants to whomever he wants to get whatever he wants and never gets in trouble for it because, in the context of the fiction, the portrait absorbs consequences for him. Yet, if the portrait didn't exist, this would still largely be true because he is so wealthy and good-looking and white. The structure of this fantasy is revealed when Dorian is confronted by James Vane, the brother of a poor young woman named Sybil whose death Dorian caused. Vane is described as a "young lad with rough brown hair" and "not so finely bred as his sister"—he is less white even, these descriptions imply, than his own immediate family members. Vane has been hunting Dorian down for years and finally encounters him outside an opium den. (Here's a tip: if you're ever looking for someone in a nineteenth-century novel, check the opium dens *first*.) When Vane confronts Dorian and announces his intentions to avenge his sister's death, Dorian successfully convinces him he has the wrong man because Sybil's murder was so very long ago—how could he be so hot and young if he were old enough to have committed the crime? And James Vane *believes* him.

Not only does the portrait allow Dorian to continue to do terrible things to other people, but the power it grants him also prevents him from ever being accountable for having done those things. Like the circular logic Mesle describes whereby "a piece of art becomes serious because a serious critic attends to it, and a critic becomes serious by tending to serious art," the power of rich whiteness is both the warrant to do and the exculpation for having done. As Dorian's friend Lord Henry says, "It is not in you, Dorian, to commit a murder. I am sorry if I hurt your vanity by saying so, but I assure you it is true. Crime belongs exclusively to the lower orders."

RWP are always getting away with murder figuratively but just as often quite literally. When someone dies accidentally (or not) in an RWPF, that person is likely to be poor and/or of color. James Vane, I should mention, dies just such a death when he is shot in a hunting accident at Dorian's country estate. The accident is viewed as a mere inconvenience, as it means the hunting must cease for the day because, as Lord Henry observes, "It would not look well to go on." In the first season of *Downton Abbey*, Lady Mary likewise finds herself having to tastefully dispose of a body. The dead guy is Mr. Pamuk, a Turkish ambassador who sneaks into her bed for some late-night entertainment after a day spent being ogled by the inhabitants of the Abbey male and female, who all appreciate his "exotic" beauty. The overriding concern of Lady Mary, her maid, and her mother—the intrepid trio who remove the body from Mary's bed—is for the preservation of her sexual virtue. There is never a whisper of a fear that Mary will be suspected of his murder. This must be what it means to feel white.

A complicated instance of a fictional RWP who does *not* get away with murder is the case of Carl Bruner—the weaselly, despicable, and perpetually sweaty white guy who hires a Brown hit man to knock off his best friend. I'm talking about the 1990 movie *Ghost*. Before moving on to the film's racial politics, a few words about the scene you're probably thinking about, the one that popularized ceramics for an entire generation. It begins with the exceptionally hot Demi Moore, working in her ceramics studio late at night wearing nothing but a man's shirt and no underwear, as one does. Anyway, she's making a beautiful, tall vase when Patrick Swayze sneaks up behind her in some tight, unbuttoned jeans to ask, "What are you doing?" This is probably the most annoying thing a man could possibly say to a woman very obviously at work. What do you think she's doing, fool? She's sitting at a pottery wheel shaping a vase, as you can see perfectly well with your squinty little eyes. What this question is really saying is, "Why are you not prioritizing our sexy time above all else?" It's a classic male inability to recognize the value of female labor, so—no surprise—he proceeds to destroy the art she has painstakingly begun, which in any other context would not be a sexy thing to do at all. In fact, she even makes a disgruntled face when he does it, and if I'd never seen the film before or the many parodies of this scene and paused it right there, I'd be pretty convinced it would be followed by a fight that went something like, "Hey, you just fucked up my vase!" But instead, of course, they make out in a supremely unrealistic fashion that involves mostly swan-like neck rubbing, and I swear this is relevant because how they make out comes up again at the end in a surprising way.

What accounts for the success of the scene as a sexy moment rather than an obnoxious example of the male sabotage of female labor and creativity is, first, the positive associations with Patrick Swayze's neck created by *Dirty Dancing* (1987); and, second, the sudden introduction of the extradiegetic soundtrack that subsequently became the "first dance" song at countless weddings, the "last dance" song at countless proms, and the first song I personally ever slow-danced to, albeit at a Lady Mary–worthy distance from my awkward date: "Unchained Melody." You know the lyrics:

> Oh, my love, my darling
> I've hungered for your touch
> A long, lonely time
> Time goes by so slowly
> And time can do so much

Are you still mine?
I need your love
I need your love
God speed your love to me
Lonely rivers flow
To the sea, to the sea
To the open arms of the sea
Lonely rivers sigh
Wait for me, wait for me
I'll be coming home, wait for me.

For the first dancers, the last dancers, and the pimpled kids in the gym, it's a song about erotic longing—the agony one feels in the even temporary absence of the beloved.

But here's something interesting: although almost all contemporary Americans will associate this song with the Righteous Brothers version featured in *Ghost*, it was originally written for a different movie, a movie about incarceration. The 1955 film *Unchained* tells the story of a white guy who is serving time in a medium-security prison from which he tries to escape in order to see his family. While he's locked up, a fellow prisoner (played by the African American actor Todd Duncan) sings the song from his bed in the cell, strumming the guitar in tortured melancholy. The camera alternates between close-ups on Duncan's face and pans of the other prisoners in their cells, who are of many different colors. Their shared circumstance of incarceration, their woeful faces imply, makes the song hit them all the same.

It makes sense, in a way, that the prison—the place where people are stripped of their humanity—is the site of their unlikely communion. This carceral logic grounds the show *Orange Is the New Black*, too. The non-white inmates on the show are televisually humanized by their contact with an unexpectedly imprisoned rich white girl named Piper. The show's creator, Jenji Kohan said in a 2013 interview with NPR's Terry Gross,

> In a lot of ways Piper was my Trojan Horse. You're not going to go into a network and sell a show on really fascinating tales of black women, and Latina women, and old women and criminals. But if you take this white girl, this sort of fish out of water, and you follow her in, you can then expand your world and tell all of those other stories. But it's a hard sell to just go in and try to sell those stories initially. The girl next door, the cool blonde, is a very easy access point, and it's relatable for a lot of audiences and a lot of networks looking for a certain demographic. It's useful.

There weren't any cool blondes next door in the Jewish neighborhood where I grew up; but I get what she's saying here, and it's even worse than it sounds. Kohan seems to be arguing that proximity to the white character allows for the visibility of the nonwhite characters. The power of Piper's whiteness is transferable in a limited way. Kohan makes "the cool blonde" the center of the story because a key project of American culture has been to teach readers and viewers that white people are subjects worth looking at, worth winning, worth loving.

Piper's whiteness, like the protagonist's whiteness in Kohan's other hit show, *Weeds*, is also important because it provides the unlikely, comedic setup for the show. *How could a suburban white lady be a drug dealer? Weeds* asks. *What if a rich, white girl had to go to prison?* ponders *Orange Is the New Black. Ghost* is also about a circumstance that is apparently hysterically unimaginable in the beginning of the nineties: that of a white man and a Black woman being friends. Like other narrative circumstances that were so unexpected as to be considered fodder for slapstick comedy in this period (What if three *men* had to raise . . . wait for it . . . a *baby*?!?!), all of the jokes in *Ghost* come from how Patrick Swayze's character, Sam, is thrown into a circumstance in which the only living person with whom he can communicate is Whoopi Goldberg's Oda Mae Brown. But Oda Mae is not just Sam's friend; she is who he must depend upon to assert his desires in the physical world. He is a white man who has to experience being invisible, and she is a Black woman who—like so many poor, dark people—has to actually do all of the work to get the desires of the white guy met, an essential worker. For this she is never thanked or even acknowledged.

In order for Sam to use Oda Mae to gratify his wish to avenge his death and murder the other white guy, Carl, he has to teach her how to access the privileges of being white. When he sends Oda Mae into the bank to withdraw the money Carl stole and placed in a dummy account, Sam coaches Oda Mae through her conversation with the executive at the desk. "Ask how Bobby and Snooky are," he whispers in her ear. "Tell him you've been wondering how they did on the Gibraltar securities." When ghost-Sam sees his wife, Molly, entering the bank and decides to follow her, he warns Oda Mae, "I'll be back in a minute. You're on your own. Don't say anything foolish." His fears about her "foolishness" are rooted in her inexperience speaking with bank executives and withdrawing large sums of money—activities that are second nature to him, activities in which he believes he had the warrant to partake. Nor does he consider how it might feel to be her in this scenario, a Black woman cast as suspicious in a white space. Neither does he think about what it might be like to be a Black woman ordering up a cashier's check for $4 million because the ghost of a rich, white man instructed you to do so and then be told you can't keep a single cent of this money even though you've put your own life in danger to get it as a part of some messed-up, white-people revenge plot that has absolutely nothing to do with you or your life.

But Oda Mae is used to not being seen or acknowledged as a full-fledged person by the dominant culture. In a scene in which she and her sisters, like Issa and friends, are watching TV, Arsenio Hall appears on-screen. "I'm Arsenio Hall," he says in the short clip. "Don't adjust your television—I'm Black." His joke addresses the hypothetical viewer's question that remains in the minds of the hypothetical viewers whom Jenji Kohan imagines watching her shows: Why are we even *seeing* a Black person represented? And then Oda Mae's sisters beg her to change the channel. "I wanna watch *Love Connection*," one says. "I love *Love Connection*. That *man* on there," presumably referring to host Chuck Woolery. The implication is that she would rather look at a white man than a Black one. Which is comedic, of course, because on *Love Connection*, people of different races are not thrown together: Oda Mae's sister's desire for this white man is just a joke. By 1990, when *Ghost* came out, there were still no interracial episodes of the show.

The interracial romantic moment in *Ghost* is not fully represented but is nevertheless present. At the end of the film, after Sam has used Oda Mae to gain intel on Carl's misdeeds, withdraw Carl's stolen money from the bank, and avenge his own death by risking hers (trashing her apartment in the process)—all without using his ghostly powers to improve her life in any tangible way (which he easily could have done through ghostly machinations I have imagined in great detail)—she offers to let him use her yet again to have one last make-out session with Molly. "Okay, okay, you can use me," she tells him. "You can use my body." And Sam's spirit inhabits her. Whoopi then begins to take Demi into her arms; but just before she does, that old soundtrack kicks in again, and for the viewers' eyes, Whoopi's body is swapped out with Swayze's.

We are gratified to watch Sam and Molly make out again to the tune of "Unchained Melody" in that same, strange swan-necking style, which makes sense because it might be more than 1990s audiences could bear if there were even the possibility of imagining Whoopi and Demi really kissing, but it's still pretty amazing to imagine what it would look like if they had left Whoopi in the scene, what with all of its sensual caresses and neck work. Ultimately, Oda Mae's body is entirely erased both by Sam's and by the hypothetical viewers' desires.

Oda Mae's erasure is something the film takes as natural, but it significantly finds its parallel in Sam's experience. He, too, now knows what it feels like to be erased. As a ghost, he has had to learn what it feels like not to own his own body. He can move things a bit, though the extreme difficulty of doing so pains him, but he can be neither seen nor heard. He cannot be freed from the prison of his own invisibility, his own status as a nonhuman human. In short, Swayze-as-Sam kind of experiences what it feels like to be nonwhite. And this aspect of the film may be part of the reason why "Swayze" has become a hip-hop term for being gone, as in Notorious B.I.G.'s rhyme "That's why I bust back, it don't faze me / When he drop, take his Glock and I'm Swayze," Method Man's "Out of her fuckin' mind, now I got mine, I'm Swayze," or the Alkaholiks' "We dropped the microphone, then we Swayze."

Death, like prison, the film seems to say, is a great equalizer. In these sites, the characters experience not only what it is to miss one's beloved but what it is to miss owning one's own body. "What I'd give to have a drag!" one of the film's other ghostly characters wails when he looks at a pile of cigarettes littered on the floor. It reminds me of a poem by Louise Glück, wherein the speaker contemplates what she will miss when she, too, is Swayze:

> My body, now that we will not be traveling
>   together much longer
> I begin to feel a new tenderness toward you,
>   very raw and unfamiliar,
> like what I remember of love when I was young—
> . . . .
> My soul has been so fearful, so violent; forgive
>   its brutality.
> As though it were that soul, my hand moves
>   over you cautiously,
>
> not wishing to give offense
> but eager, finally, to achieve expression as
>   substance:

> it is not the earth I will miss,
> it is you I will miss.

In the thought and fear of death, we grieve for our own bodies. And the social death of having a body that the dominant culture must erase is an experience of death before death, of inhabiting the earth as a ghost. "I am an invisible man," the protagonist of Ralph Ellison's 1952 novel tells us. "No, I am not a spook like those who haunted Edgar Allan Poe; nor am I one of your Hollywood-movie ectoplasms. I am a man of substance, of flesh and bone, fiber and liquids—and I might even be said to possess a mind. I am invisible, understand, simply because people refuse to see me."

RWPFs allow readers and viewers to grieve the invisibility of the nonwhite body, the loss of the self and the right to exist in their own worlds with power and freedom. At the same time, such fictions also offer the fantasy of what it would be like to be seen, to be heard, to be able to make things move effortlessly. They often do this through the metaphor of love, because what is love but empowerment? To be really and truly loved is the fulfillment of the desire to be seen for who you are, to be treated with care and respect.

> I've hungered for your touch
> A long, lonely time
> Time goes by so slowly

And time can do so much
Are you still mine?
I need your love
I need your love
God speed your love to me.

This is a dirge of the meantime, of the promise of love that may never be met and the validation of a fierce and patient desire.

3

SAYING YES TO THE DRESS

But so absorbing is the experience of shame that it prompts the wish to disappear, to not be there. There is the unbearable attention to the self, and then the murder, the vanishing act of the mortified self. . . . Shame is the ethnic cleansing of the self. It is a state of horrified and horrifying conviction. It is the making of a dreaded spectacle of oneself.

—Adam Phillips

If you were an alien watching the culture streamed from Earth, you might reasonably conclude that getting left at the altar is a hideous rite of passage for adult American women. When Carrie Bradshaw's groom, whom she disturbingly calls "Big" (as if Black Donalding him with language alone), tells her that he won't walk down the aisle on their elaborate wedding day, she beats him about the head with her bouquet. Petals scatter all over the street while she shouts, "I am humiliated!" And it occurs to me in this climactic moment of the *Sex and the City* movie (2008) that the only thing more humiliating than walking down an aisle in a gigantic white dress while everyone gawks at you is *not* walking down an aisle in a gigantic white dress while everyone gawks at you if that is what you had intended on doing. Carrie has become, as Adam Phillips writes, a dreaded spectacle. What was supposed to be the best day of her life is now the worst, and the enormity of the dress she wears both symbolizes and emphasizes this cruel twist.

No other garment is possessed of such formidable power and cultural baggage as the wedding dress, a fixture in a range of guilty pleasure media and equally at home in romance, humor, and horror. The wedding dress encases its wearer behind layers of structural fabric as the veil obscures her face. In guilty pleasure stories, the wedding dress is typically presented as a tantalizing luxury but in ways that show that the luxury isn't something the woman has; it is something she is. The wedding dress is the complete realization of woman-made-property. This is and isn't a problem—in narrativizing the problem, guilty pleasure media repurpose that problem for its own ends. (Spoiler: those ends are about love but not in the way you may be thinking.)

The femme's relationship to this wearable object is distinct from the bonnet that gets tossed or the bodice that gets ripped. The wedding dress is sacrosanct: preserved for the next generation to wear, taking up more space in the bride's closet than her body would. It's different, too, from the body and the brace or the face and the "face." Those crutches work in tandem with the specific woman to produce a hybrid body that is both self and society, pleasure and shame. The wedding dress replaces her entirely. A common trope of the wedding film is a joke about how the bride is lost within the dress: it works at odds with the body. A bride is a changeable thing, or rather a static thing that varies only in who gets to be one at any given time. Oftentimes a woman will wear the dress her mother wore before her. Once inside of the dress, the woman *becomes* the bride—she is swallowed by the enormity of the dress's physical and cultural significance. This is exactly what happens to Carrie Bradshaw.

The *Sex and the City* movie is neither the best wedding-dress movie nor the worst nor the most famous. But it may indeed be the *most* wedding-dress movie, as it features a veritable smorgasbord of fabulous wedding dresses and wedding-dress plot points, which is why I discuss it here. In the beginning of the movie, Carrie chooses what she'll wear to her wedding herself: an elegantly tailored vintage suit. But then Carrie tries on a whole array of designer wedding dresses at the behest of her editor, who invites her to be photographed for a feature called "The Last Single Girl" because, as the editor says, "Forty is the last age a woman can be photographed in a wedding dress without the unintended Diane Arbus subtext." This line is horrifying because it's mostly true.

It's hard to think of an older bride all decked out in bridal whites without thinking of Dickens's Miss Havisham from *Great Expectations* (1860), that devastating caricature of the female body gone to rot like an old bride cake. Dickens's narrator, Pip, reflects of the decaying bride, "I saw that the dress had been put upon the rounded figure of a young woman, and that the figure upon which it now hung loose had shrunk to skin and bone." Havisham is a mutable figure within the static edifice of *the dress*, the fancy packaging that most signals her propertyness. She is also stuck at her left-at-the-altar moment: the dress cements her status as an unused object.

Once Carrie is invited to the *Vogue* shoot, all of her fantasies of a simple wedding "without the Arbusian subtext" fly out the window. Suddenly she is cast into a variety of different roles and environments: there is the Vera Wang situation, in which she figures as a kind of tulle shrubbery against a background of green florals; the Christian LaCroix situation, in which she twirls behind a '20s-era dressing screen, pearls dripping down her back; the Lanvin confection that has her looking like a Charlotte Russe set out for tea in a cherry orchard; the terrifyingly hatted Dior number that gets set in a chateau-like boudoir and reminds me of nothing so much as imprisonment, an impression enhanced by her visibly limited ability to breathe within it; and finally the Vivienne Westwood dress that, as Carrie narrates, is "so special it could bring a wedding tear to even the most unbelieving." At this insight, the camera shifts to her friend Samantha, the most antiwedding member of her female coterie, who is wiping a single tear from her warmly grinning cheek.

Samantha's dramatic tear signals how the wedding dress has the power to move even the most skeptical femme. Between the discomfort, the virginal color choice, and the heavy-handed symbolism all around, the big, white dress is easily recognizable as both a symbol and a tool of patriarchal oppression. And yet, and yet. Some of the most ardent feminists I know have lost weeks of sleep debating between dresses, made heavily populated Pinterest boards for the purpose of fantasizing about dresses, and cried while being laboriously buttoned into the folds of "the one." On the reality show *Say Yes to the Dress*, which is entirely about the emotionally fraught process of wedding-dress shopping, the assembled group of the bride's friends and family regularly burst into paroxysms of distress and joy over decisions regarding lace and sheer panels, trains and seam placement. Really, the wedding dress is the pièce de résistance of guilty pleasure objects.

In the 1994 film *Muriel's Wedding*, Toni Collette's awkward Muriel indulges in a secret passion for photographing herself in wedding dresses at bridal stores, amassing an album of Polaroids of herself as a blushing bride. It's a devastatingly embarrassing plot point but nevertheless makes me like Muriel even more. The aspect of the wedding she's drawn to is the fantasy of being picked. "When will it be me?" she sighs repeatedly throughout the film, which communicates that her desire for love is so great that it manifests as a wish to be publicly celebrated by anybody and everybody. She doesn't care whom she marries (and indeed ends up marrying an Olympic-hopeful swimmer looking for an easy path to an Australian visa). Her concern is that she gets to wear the dress, gets to be the center of attention for the precise reason of having been chosen as desirable. I never lose sympathy for Muriel because she herself understands her desires as embarrassing—not only the album of dresses she hides under her bed but also her obsessive love of the music of ABBA, which she eventually comes to embrace through her friendship with Rhonda, played by the fabulous Rachel Griffiths. Rhonda's shared love of ABBA releases Muriel from her shameful dependence on their music. "When I lived in Porpoise Spit," she tells Rhonda after a fight, "I'd just stay in my room for hours and listen to ABBA songs. Sometimes I'd stay in there all day. But since I've met you and moved to Sydney, I haven't listened to one ABBA song. It's because now my life's as good as an ABBA song. It's as good as 'Dancing Queen.'" Muriel comes to find, in the end, that Rhonda's love is more fulfilling than the groom and gauzy folds she'd been so long dreaming of.

Female buddy movies like *Muriel's Wedding* often center around the duo's shared consumption of femme cultural objects. And just as often as this co-consumption is a celebration, it is also a roast. Like the characters in *Insecure* or the groups of women across the country hosting *Bachelor* watch parties with a deeply unclear degree of irony, we make fun of our media together as a form of bonding. Lately a term has developed for this practice: "hate-watching." We hate-watch because it represents the conflicted way in which we love because we've been taught to love under a system that, ultimately, hates us. At the beginning of the 1997 buddy comedy *Romy and Michele's High School Reunion*, we see the titular duo hate-watching *Pretty Woman*:

> Michele: You know, even though we've watched *Pretty Woman*, like, thirty-six times, I never get tired of making fun of it.
>
> Romy: Oh, I know. Aw, poor thing. Look, they won't let her shop. Yeah, like those salesgirls in Beverly Hills aren't bigger whores than she is.
>
> Michele: I know!
>
> Romy: Oh, my God, listen to that sad, sad music as she leaves.
>
> Michele: It's like, boo-hoo. Ugh! But it is, actually, kind of sad.

Both funny and sad, bitter and loving, our mocking of femme fictions is how we adore them. It's also how we adore weddings. Everyone loves to complain about them, to criticize the choices and demands made, the clichéd speeches. But weddings are also very fun to attend. They make us cry; they make us dance; they are an all-ages social event.

While the vast majority of romcoms are about the search for heterosexual romantic love, wedding movies, as the theorist Elizabeth Freeman points out, tend to be about the solidification of queer bonds and identities. So it makes sense that the focus of the wedding plot of the *Sex and the City* movie, as in the series, is the friend group, not the marriage— the chosen family, not the biological one. This has the paradoxical impact of solidifying queer kinship structures over normative ones. And it's a feature of almost all wedding movies, a point to which I'll shortly return, but first I have to explain how the queer liberatory potential of the wedding film has quite a bit to do with the structures of property and ownership at the center of the wedding ritual.

Big and Carrie decide to get married because they are planning to move in together, and Carrie's concern is that, if he doesn't put a ring on it, she will have no legal rights to their collective apartment if or when things go south. Both the casualness of the conversation and the practicality of their reasons for making things "official" seem to be positioned as a modern, progressive take on the whole institution. They will have their security and their freedom from fustiness too. "Should I get you a diamond?" Big asks over the kitchen counter. "No, no," Carrie says, "just get me a really big closet." Despite all of this superficial modern casualness, Carrie's centering her marriage decision on property—both the apartment and the closet, the place where she'll store all those Louboutin pumps that the show made famous (Carrie was ahead of Cardi in celebrating "these expensive, these is red bottoms, these is bloody shoes")—lands her squarely in the very long tradition of wedding rites.

Weddings, as you probably know, have always been about the exchange of goods. (And I'm not just talking land mergers and Neiman Marcus registries here.) The anthropologist Margaret Mead compiled a list of the sayings of the Arapesh of New Guinea, one of which is "Your own mother, your own sister, your own pigs, your own yams that you have piled up, you may not eat. Other people's mothers, other people's sisters, other people's pigs, other people's yams that they have piled up, you may eat." In short, a gift of a bride is no different from a gift of yams: the recipient takes into his home and consumes a thing that was given, not something he himself cultivated, and this seals the relationship between the two groups. Women, yams—it doesn't matter which—are gifts to be given for the purpose of formalizing property relations. This is why the father of the bride must give her away. It's a vestige of the practice of exchange between men that says *what's mine is yours, what's yours is mine.* It's not really the precious-metal rings at the heart of the wedding exchange; it's the woman.

While it's true that under most current legal systems, marriage grants women the combined ownership of their husbands' property, it's also true that marriage was created as a system wherein women themselves are the property exchanged. This has real consequences for its present-day iteration, no matter how casual or modern the approach. We can't rid the marriage system of the legacy of women-as-property. It's just built that way. And the wedding dress most clearly communicates not only the property status of women but also a way of assessing their value. The more expensive and elaborate the dress—indeed the more expensive and elaborate the wedding—the more value is ascribed to the woman to be found somewhere inside it.

This is why women fantasize about the wedding despite their abject yam-like role within it: women are always treated as property, and at least in the scene of the wedding, more than anywhere else, they become visible and valued as what they are. This is also why Carrie is so humiliated to be left at the altar: despite all of the apparent value of her as a bride, Big will not seal the deal. Viewers of the movie will remember that after being left, Carrie writes off Big altogether until she returns to the gorgeous penthouse apartment they would have shared. It's the last day before the new owners take possession of the place, and Carrie goes to retrieve a pair of unworn stilettos that lie in wait in the enormous closet Big had built especially for her. And there, in this closet that magically created space (it is somehow at least ten times the size of the original closet, although nothing else seems altered by the renovation), Carrie encounters Big for the first time since his betrayal. Inexplicably, she rushes into his arms and kisses him. "It wasn't logic," her voice-over says. "It was love." Cut to a postcoital moment in the same closet presumably minutes later, where Carrie reflects, "It's a good closet. It's comfortable." And then she accepts his second marriage proposal, while they are still inside this improbably large and apparently very comfortable windowless room made for the storage of valuable goods.

There's a symmetry to Carrie's proposal acceptance within a closet because, in some sense, Carrie spent the entire beloved series living in one. Carrie's pre-Big apartment is basically one giant closet around a smaller closet. She quips that she keeps sweaters in her stove, and the big "I'm finally moving out!" scene (one of the film's most pleasurable moments) is a fashion show she puts on for her girlfriends in order to decide what clothing to keep and what clothing to jettison before transitioning to her grown-up married life. Part of the pleasure to be found in the scene for viewers is the reminiscing that goes with her various outfits. Each ensemble recalls a different romantic relationship she weathered in the series's episodes. The outfits are representative of the different lives she could have had with the different men she dated: lewks and circumstances into which her body is inserted.

Carrie's single, city-girl lifestyle reminds me of one of my favorite childhood toys: a carrier for a Barbie doll that was also a stage set for Barbie play. The carrier was shaped like a cylinder that could be unfolded to reveal two separate scenes, one on each side. Inside was an apartment with a single Murphy bed where Barbie slept that also contained a closet in which to hang her outfits—my favorite feature. The outside of the carrier was an office with a Murphy desk. This Barbie, apparently, only worked and slept. I would think of her often in graduate school. As a child, when I wasn't playing with Barbie, I could close her up inside the apartment set and put her away in the larger closet of the carrier, as I had her put her clothes away in the smaller closet inside it. The Barbie in the carrier is a lot like the turning ballerina that folds into the jewelry box, which so many little girls are also given. (I had the jewelry box, too, and mine even played a few bars of Tchaikovsky's "Dying Swan" theme to be extra depressing—but how I loved her!) In fact, countless toys aimed at girl children center on the theme of a female body encased in a compartment for the storage of property: there is Polly Pocket, a small doll that comes shut up in various purses and compacts alongside her accessories; Shopkins, which I don't really understand but seem to be partially edible girls enclosed in "lil' secret playsets"; and so on and so forth.

One way we know women are culturally cast as property is the way in which we fantasize about being stored among our goods. I call this trope the "femme closet fantasy" or, when I'm feeling more feisty, "vagina rooms." We don't yet have an epistemology of the straight female closet, the place where we contend with the fraught desires of female heterosexuality without the oppressive presence of their objects. Closeted women are removed from the humiliating spectacle of their own desire without having to be cursed to sleep, fairy-tale-like, for the rest of their days. There is no pleasure in hiding in a closet without the added comfort of the femme objects contained therein, which caress the closeted woman with the accoutrements of her own body rather than the demands of everyone else's. (Reading itself can be a kind of femme closet, a way of hiding from such demands in plain sight while dwelling in femme pleasures invisible to the outside world.)

There's a classic femme closet fantasy at the end of *The Wide, Wide World*—you remember, that nineteenth-century sentimental coming-of-age romance in which Ellen Montgomery marries her brother/lover, the horsewhipper-cum-clergyman John Humphreys. In the novel, John leaves Ellen to her disagreeable Scottish relatives for a while before finally coming to retrieve her and bring her back to America to be his bride. The novel published in the nineteenth century ends there, but for reasons unknown to scholars, Warner wrote an additional chapter that was never published in her lifetime, which we usually read as the ending of the novel today. This second, additional ending is the ultimate fantasy of submission, domestic bliss, and—to take a page from *Sex and the City*'s Carrie—comfortable and spacious closets.

When John takes Ellen home as his bride, he leads her to a secret new room beyond his own study, a room that is her room, and already prefilled with all of the possessions she might desire, where "nothing had been spared which wealth could provide or taste delight in, or curious affection contrive for its object." He has decorated her inner sanctum with statuary and paintings in feminine themes, fine goods and furnishings, and even an "escritoire" filled with cash! A lovely thing herself, Ellen is placed in a room for the storage of lovely and valuable things—like Carrie in the closet to be filled with designer shoes and handbags, my Barbie tucked secretly inside her carrying-case apartment, or the ballerina who, when the box is closed and she is not made to dance, can relax among pink velvet folds stuffed with rings and bracelets. (You can see why I tend to associate these spaces with the vaginal.)

The status of brides as consumable goods is quite clear here in the sense that, like precious goods, they are to be taken out and played with at the whim of their possessor, then locked away again in their closet when they are not in use. But this is not by any means a male-authored fantasy of female oppression. The fantasy of Ellen in her closet room is Warner's, the fantasy of Carrie getting fucked on the comfortable closet carpet presumably Carrie's, and the fantasy of the Barbie who can be tucked away like her clothes or the ballerina with her jewels mine.

Women locked away with their valuables, when I put it this way, may seem a purely dark and awful vision, but there's catharsis in these closeted female figures. The fantasy is not about what happens when we take them out, I think; it's about what it means that they get to spend most of their time shut in: the closet offers a welcome break from it all.

This is particularly valuable as an outcome in the context of the wedding and the marriage that follows, in which women are not only the commodity but also the brokers of the deal and the facilitators of the event. This triple status is, like everything else about women's lives, extremely exhausting. What the closet offers is not just confirmation of our own commodity status. Even better, the closet offers invisibility and rest, a chance to be completely closed off, no longer open for business. (Another place we find this is the late-sixties sitcom *I Dream of Jeannie*, in which the beleaguered housewife who is also a magical genie captured by her astronaut/"master"/husband retreats to her cloistered bottle, a kind of Orientalist magical closet that also deeply resembles a vagina.) These women find relief in being put away in a closet like The Dress itself after the mass spectacle of a wedding, a spectacle that benefits practically every other person present far more than it benefits the person for whom it is supposed to be the best imaginable day—the bride at its center.

The trouble for modern-day brides is that their existence as inert exchange object is no longer sufficient. They cannot merely be yams. Carrie laments her left-at-the-altar street scene with Big, telling her friends, "After ten years of what he already put me through, he couldn't make the effort and get out of the car. I made the effort. I put a bird on my head," referring to the fascinator she added to the Westwood veil to make it "hers." (Here we continue in the long tradition of women with embarrassing things on their heads.) Today's bride is both the architect of the deal and the object of exchange. "I am humiliated!" Carrie yells at Big not only because she's been rejected but also because she went to the trouble of planning an entire wedding down to the last ridiculous detail of a bird on top of her head and he couldn't even be bothered to attend.

In a 2018 *Washington Post* article, the wedding advice columnist Liz Moorhead describes how she's noticed a disturbing backlash to the "bridezilla" trope. Bridezillas, mind you, are the demanding brides who ask too much of their friends and family, rack up exorbitant bills, and yell at everyone for no reason. They are the entertaining focus of the reality show of the same name, of the 2009 romcom *Bride Wars*, of the teary shouting matches on *Say Yes to the Dress*. Bridezillas are the illusion of bridal power gone bad. The wedding is their one big day, the only time they will perceive themselves to be the focus of everyone's admiration and attention, so it has to be perfect—and they will stop at nothing to make it so.

Of course, "bridezillas" are make-believe. They are a fictional way of chastising women for wanting any power at all, however illusory. The true reality, as Moorhead points out, is that there are two sides to land on within the confines of this suffocating bridezilla stereotype: one is to be so extremely stressed out by the demands of executing her own wedding that, yes, the bride becomes irritable and unhappy. For shame! The other is to be "the laid-back bride" who grossly overcorrects this behavior so as to avoid seeming bridezilla-y. The "laid-back bride," a nuptial version of Gillian Flynn's "cool girl," must do not only all of the labor of planning the wedding but also the labor of hiding that labor and its emotional wages to avoid being cast in the bridezilla role. "A 'bridezilla,'" Moorhead writes,

> often enough, is handling things in a completely normal way. It's not like the chill, "laid-back bride" has less to shoulder by pretending she doesn't care or by becoming an emotionless robot. She has all the more pressure in facing those same problems without letting it show: She's still feeding 150 people, confirming there's a ramp for Grandma's wheelchair and making sure all the guests are happy, whether she admits it's an elaborate production or not. The wedding doesn't just have to look nice or be meaningful, as it did six years ago. It has to avoid inconveniencing a soul.

The bride is not the center of the wedding in the way an attendee at one's own surprise birthday gathering is the center of the party; she is the center of the wedding in the way a hog is the center of a pig roast—but if the hog also had to cook itself. This is because, while marriage as an institution is the place within society where heteronormative roles are most enforced, the wedding has actually very little to do with the couple around whom it is centered. The wedding is often the first (and will sometimes be the only) time a couple's friends and family all meet each other. The event instantiates a new kinship group and sanctions a new merger of social circles. Creating this event is the bride's job.

For this reason, a lot of wedding movies are also RWPFs or fictions centered on overcoming race and class conflict through marriage. The wedding film classic *My Big, Fat Greek Wedding* (2002) tells the story of how the superwhite groom, played by John Corbett of *Sex and the City* and *Northern Exposure* fame, adapts to accommodate his super-Greek bride-to-be's family. The beginning of the movie is all about how Toula, played by Nia Vardalos, could never possibly hope to attract any man because she is thirty and Greek. The middle of the movie is all about how she can't believe that such a white man likes her. And the end of the movie is all about how some boring WASPs (John Corbett and his parents) find Greek people to be surprisingly "fun," mostly because they drink ouzo, which is delicious. Though I thoroughly enjoy this film because of Andrea Martin's performance as Aunt Voula and the mere presence of Joey Fatone, I don't agree with any of these premises, including that ouzo is delicious. But the point here is that the wedding itself is completely for the families, and when John Corbett agrees to get shirtless Greek-baptized with a lot of oils and water (I do agree with this part), it's not out of love for Toula, who actually proposes that they elope, but out of adherence to the idea that the wedding is far more about solidifying familial bonds than it is about sexual or romantic love.

One thing that's very weird about the *Sex and the City* movie (I mean there are a lot of weird things, but let me try to focus here) is that though Carrie is getting married in a big ceremony at the New York Public Library (the biggest femme book closet in the world) with all of her friends and acquaintances in attendance, no one ever breathes so much as a word about her family. Since the wedding never happens, we don't know who would have walked her down the aisle, but there is no mention of a father or a mother, siblings, cousins, or grandparents. This is true of the entire series, in fact.* Where *is* Carrie's family? Why is their existence erased so entirely that I can only imagine her birth as an image of her springing out of a New York City sewer grate as a fully formed adult woman carrying a Birkin bag and a big, honk-ing nineties laptop?

This elaborate omission in the series is a plot structure similar to the nineteenth-century novel

---

* Okay, I am aware that they are briefly alluded to in season 2, but they are never seen.

trope of the orphan or innocent thrust alone into the wide, wide world—a master plot that the literary critic Lionel Trilling called "the young man from the provinces," the story of a rural rube who sets out to conquer the big city. The entire *Sex and the City* series loves this trope so much that the beginning of the movie rehearses it: "Year after year," Carrie's voice-over intones in the film's very first spoken words, "twenty-something women come to New York City in search of the two Ls: labels and love." This is a feminized version of the provincial-young-man myth. While he wants to create a career and collect a wife, she wants to shop and be collected by a husband (then, presumably, stored in some kind of precious container). At any rate, the real treasure that Carrie unexpectedly finds is her friends. Instead of focusing on the protagonist's linear quest for love with poorly drawn friends serving mostly as comic relief and thin subplot fodder, as many femme fictions of its period did, *Sex and the City* focused squarely on the relationships between the female ensemble cast members—love interests came and went and rarely provided emotionally satisfying story arcs.

But wedding movies have long traded in ensemble casts and friendship drama. The 1999 wedding-movie classic *The Best Man*, for example, is about a group of college friends who all come back together when a couple from among them finally decides to get married. The wedding is referred to by multiple characters as a "wedding/reunion," and it is made almost explicit that the entire point of this wedding is to reunite the mixed-gender friend group, whose bonds have become frayed by distance and the demands of their professional lives (like the *Sex and the City* ladies, most of them are improbably successful: a television producer, an Oprah's book-club novelist, an NFL player, etc.).

The film is anchored by the hotness of the main character, Harper (played by Taye Diggs), the novelist whose most recent work is a roman à clef of the friend group's adventures in college, notably the sexual exploits of the groom-to-be, Lance, the now-pro football player. What Harper's novel also reveals is that, in college, Harper once slept with the bride-to-be, Mia. (Why anyone would write this kind of novel is a question unanswered.) This is an especially big deal because Lance believes that, despite his own numerous sexual adventures, he is the only person with whom the chaste and serious Mia has ever had sex. Once Lance figures out the truth by reading the novel the night before the wedding, the film's central conflict emerges, and the friend group is threatened because, among other things, Lance literally tries to murder Harper.

The resolution of the conflict (another friend intercepts the attempted murder, and then all is basically well) is Lance's acceptance that, like men, women have sexual desire and maybe it's not a terrible thing for his wife to have had another sexual partner at some point, even if that partner is his best friend. The scene wherein Lance and Mia exchange vows at the actual wedding ceremony is interspersed with flashbacks to the college-era sexual encounter between Mia and Harper. In between the tearful words Lance speaks aloud about his eternal love for God and his bride-to-be, Mia is shown being taken from behind by the best man. And it's actually kind of moving—the message being that Lance loves her, past and all. The wedding, which you might think would be about solidifying the exclusive sexual partnership of its protagonists, is here recast as an expression of communal bonds through the revelation of infidelity. It's worth pointing out, however, that the bride remains the object of exchange that these two men use to reaffirm their connection to each other.

The Best Man is a somewhat rare film, for its moment, in that it focuses on the male half of the wedding party more so than the female half. But the one really developed female character within it is also the only character who remains outside a heterosexual pair bond at the end, the television producer Jordan, whom the men, in conversation with one another, describe as "half lesbian" because she has seemingly no need for a male partner. As Freeman also describes, the queer figure is a staple in wedding depictions—the gay wedding planner, the "half lesbian" friend, the gay best friend, the queer sexual exploits at the bachelor or bachelorette party.

Many wedding movies, like *The Best Man*, focus entirely on the wedding's peripheral characters—the group of friends and/or family who rally to support the bride and groom. The protagonist of the 2011 film *Bridesmaids* is the maid of honor, Annie, played by Kristen Wiig, a woman whose singleness is cast as a perpetual problem. One of the other bridesmaids, Becca, played by Ellie Kemper, is introduced in a scene in which she shames Annie for not having a husband. By the film's end, Becca has discovered the sexual inadequacy of her own heterosexual marriage and acted on her attraction to another bridesmaid. Queer sex—be it same gender, multiple partner, or fetish sexuality—is a staple feature of hilariously "out-of-control" weddings in the genre.

When queer love is not explicitly present on the periphery of wedding movies, it is covertly at their centers. It would take only the slightest nudge to make the mostly heterosexist 2009 comedy *Bride Wars* explicitly about lesbian love. Perhaps the most bridezilla-y bridezilla film, *Bride Wars* tells the story of Liv and Emma, best friends who have long dreamed of their perfect wedding days. The beginning of the film shows them as children, play-marrying each other, with Emma always in the part of the groom. As adults, they end up unwittingly planning their weddings at the same time. Since they've developed their wedding fantasies together, they share them. This creates a conflict of interest (they want the same venue on the same day) so great that it threatens to tear apart their friendship irrevocably. But ultimately, having their weddings in separate rooms in the same venue on the same day leads to a dramatic and conflict-laden merger of the two events, with the end result being, as usual, that their weddings are about their relationship to each other far more so than about their romances with the boring, barely depicted grooms. When Emma realizes that her groom is a selfish jerk who doesn't deserve her, she actually calls off her own wedding and heads toward a relationship with Liv's brother—it's hardly a stretch to see that this is a substitution for Liv herself, the real focus of Emma's passion and erotic attention. As in the romcom of antagonists (see *The Ugly Truth* [2009], *27 Dresses* [2008], *Laws of Attraction* [2004], *How to Lose a Guy in Ten Days* [2003], etc.) where the "I hate him!" trope at the beginning of the film nearly always signals their sexual union at the end, female conflicts in wedding films are about the erotic bonds between women.

Same-sex or queer friendships provide the majority of the feel-good moments in these plots. Queerness is cast as the respite from the outrageous demands of the wedding and the oppressiveness of the heterosexuality it celebrates. The mixed-gender friend group at the heart of *Four Weddings and a Funeral* (1994) is shocked when one of them unexpectedly dies at a wedding. Their surprise is not really about his death, however; it's about how they never stopped to realize that all the time they thought they were a big ol' group of fun-loving singles, two among them were, "for all intents and purposes, married."

Gareth's funeral is the most memorable, and the only truly emotional, part of the film because it doesn't involve Andie McDowell (who is a wooden puppet) and, primarily, because of the speech made by Gareth's loving partner, Matthew, which culminates in a reading of Auden's "Funeral Blues":

> He was my north, my south, my east and west,
> my working week and my Sunday rest.
> My noon, my midnight, my talk, my song.
> I thought that love would last forever. I was wrong.

(I'm not crying; you are.) Maybe it's Matthew and Gareth's queerness that prevented their friends from noticing they were in a loving, committed relationship the whole time. But I think it's more likely because of their happiness. The rest of the eccentrically jaded friend group here associate weddings and marriage itself with a sham of love, a culturally mandated power struggle between two individuals who are forced by external factors to cohabitate and reproduce. Gareth and Matthew's relationship reads more like friendship to them not because both partners are men but because it actually seems emotionally fulfilling. Fredric Jameson (and Slavoj Žižek more famously—that guy is always stealing someone else's horse) quipped that, judging by popular culture, it's easier to imagine the apocalypse than it is to imagine the end of capitalism.* The same seems true of the heteropatriarchy. The straights in this movie can't imagine the outside of heterosexuality. And even though straight sex can be pretty pleasurable, like capitalism, heterosexuality thoroughly sucks for everyone involved.

It also seems true that it's been an even longer road for our culture to accept the pleasures of friendship than it has for same-sex romantic love. As Aminatou Sow and Ann Friedman have recently diagnosed, our culture lacks even a clear vocabulary for the kinds of love they identify as "Big Friendship": "When the world failed to provide a label for something we were experiencing as friends," they write, "we often supplied our own words for it. We came up with our own shorthand for the powerful decision to invest in our friends the way we invest in ourselves. . . . We even lacked a name for the kind of friendship we have. Words like 'best friend' or 'BFF' don't capture the adult emotional work we've put into this relationship. We now call it a Big Friendship, because it's one of the most affirming—and most complicated—relationships that a human life can hold." I felt so validated reading these words after years of struggling to explain to others what my closest friends mean to me, how inextricable the stakes

---

* If you're interested in the whole Žižek/Jameson quote debacle, see Mark Fisher's take in *Capitalist Realism*. Fisher writes, "so often is Žižek cited in connection with this dictum that some ill-informed commentators even ascribe it to him."

of my own life are from the stakes of theirs. I've often felt childish saying "my best friend" or "my childhood friend" as a means of communicating the kind of bond I share with the women who are closest to me, and in part this is because the fictions that celebrate these bonds tend to be about children: we are Anne and Diana, Kristy and Mary Anne, Jesse and Leslie, Scout and Dill. These love relationships have given me all the satisfaction of a rich, white Alice or Annie. Like Muriel, I failed to acknowledge my own gratification of that desire for a long time simply because, as a culture, we've spun our adult femme narratives so tightly around the arc of sexual love.

If romance plots and RWPFs are about the catharsis of being dominated, wedding fictions are about the catharsis of being permitted to celebrate the bond we share with equals—the kinds of love that happen outside the heterosexual pair bond that is their empty center. Contrary to the clichés—*always a bridesmaid!*—it is much more fun, in my opinion, to be a bridesmaid than a bride. And the depictions of bridesmaids are also more fun than the depictions of brides. Bridesmaids are the quirky best-friend characters—always the most interesting—moved center stage. Wedding movies allow for ensemble casts and themes of communality rather than individualism. When depictions do center on the brides themselves, they tend to lean into the bridezilla trope. But even these fictions—about the competition between mean girls—are in the end also about female reconciliation and the centrality of friendship to the emotional structure of femme lives.

Just as we mock the fictions that depict and define us, we're sometimes mean to one another because the erotics of female friendships are so powerful and taboo. The "mean girl" trope is ubiquitous in femme fictions and often tied to weddings. Contestants on *The Bachelor* compete to be the one standing beside the groom in the same spirit of bridal rage as Jane Austen heroines or the two female characters at the center of the 1997 film *My Best Friend's Wedding*. But just as insistently as these plots of female cattiness and competition are deployed, they are undermined.

Mean girls are afraid of love. Their friendships are organized as a bulwark against it. Mean girls take the pain and danger of female heterosexual desire and reverse it, like a cartoon superhero who deflects the villain's laser beam with her shield. But the lasers rebound in all directions. Speaking of flipping it and reversing it, in Missy Eliot's song "Gossip Folks," which is about mean girls (the video is set in a high school!), she raps, "How you studyin' these ho's, need to talk what you know, and stop talking 'bout who I'm sticking and licking, just mad it ain't yours. I know ya'll poor, ya'll broke, ya'll job just hanging up clothes." While Missy is ostensibly hating her haters, she's also identifying the shared structural problems at the root of their animosity. Who is to blame for their brokeness and loneliness? Certainly not Missy, as she points out. There's a compassion at the heart of her insult: she knows they're just taking out their own frustrations on her.

The negativity of the femme situation under patriarchy is the air the mean girl breathes, but, as in bodice-ripper romances, the antagonism between mean girls also has an erotic charge. We love to praise *The Golden Girls* as a classic depiction of platonic female love (which, fair, because that show was light-years ahead of its time—to the lanai!), but, let's be honest, those "girls" can be straight mean to each other. There's a ton of fat-shaming and jealousy and sabotage and classic mean-girl behavior throughout the series. To me, this seems like how they blow off steam about the pressures of an external world in which they figure as a highly invisible category of beings: aging women. The conflicts that this behavior creates also provide, as in the romcom, opportunities for passionate reconciliation—I'd conservatively estimate that about 60 percent of *Golden Girls* episodes end in a group hug and a reaffirmation of their friendship vows.

The real love story of *My Best Friend's Wedding* isn't that of Julia Roberts's character, Julianne, and her romantic interest (the guy who's supposed to be her "best friend") or that of Julianne and her male, gay other best friend (though that's pretty good, too)—it's the relationship between Julianne and her supposed rival, Cameron Diaz's Kim. The movie's most heartwarming scene takes place in a women's restroom, which is also where the movie's best knock-down, drag-out fight takes place between the same two characters. (The restroom is another version of the closet—the place where women go to cease being on display, to collect themselves and strategize together.) "He loves you," Julianne says sweetly to Kim, kissing the top of her head. "Hell, even I love you." The woman Julianne set out to "destroy," as she articulates at the beginning of the film, becomes her friend, her compatriot in the insanity of womanhood. The arc of their journey mirrors the fight-until-they-fuck drama of more conventional romantic fare, but with all of the inequity stripped away. Kim doesn't need to tame Julianne's vitriol or civilize her; Julianne arrives at a place of compassion on her own.

The depiction of female friendships is probably my favorite part of wedding films; and perhaps my favorite wedding film of all time is not about a wedding at all, but taking a page from *The Best Man*, I nevertheless think of it this way—a wedding/reunion without the wedding. I'm talking about *Romy and Michele's High School Reunion* again, a pure celebration of lady love and satire of the conventions of heterosexual romance. Romy and Michele are a delightfully quirky duo from Tucson who have lived together in domestic bliss in LA, despite their outwardly unsuccessful (no great jobs, no husbands) lives, for the past ten years. The prospect of attending their reunion sends them into a squall of feelings of inadequacy. Weddings frequently do this in film and real life, too, and that's also part of the reason why I think of this movie in this way. At any rate, by the end of the movie, they've shown all the popular girls (a trio of pregnant half-wits locked in the prison of heteronormativity) how patently superior they are, inspired the intellectual loner (played by Janeane Garofalo) to follow her own sexual passion, and garnered the sartorial approval of a *Vogue* fashion editor for the very outfits the half-wits mocked. But the best of all is the scene wherein the nerdy boy—now an RWP—who loved Michele back in the day invites her to dance with him in front of the assembled high school class. "Only if Romy can dance with us," Michele says. And to Cyndi Lauper's "Time after Time," the three perform an interpretative dance that is as much about self-expression as it is about communal love. I laugh, I cry, I make dramatic arm gestures with my besties watching beside me. This is nothing short of the "first dance" of the wedding reimagined. It erases the tragedy of the other wedding films— the bride being whisked away from her girls by the always-more-boring husband. In this version, they get to dance together (and, I suppose, with him, too).

More recent female buddy and ensemble comedic films and series like *Broad City*, *Booksmart*, *Dead to Me*, *Big Little Lies*, *Jane the Virgin*, *Pen15*, and *Insecure* bring the most significant love affairs of women's lives—those they have with each other—to the center of their stories and, for the most part, eliminate the mean-girl baggage. But we wouldn't have these fictions without the often deeply troubling romance plots that long preceded them and the equally long convention of consuming those plots with an infectious combination of admiration and disdain, love and hate, guilt and pleasure. The deep-love/surface-hate way guilty pleasures are viewed and processed mirrors the way in which women embark on the competition that our culture keeps trying to say should define our lives: in a spirit of mutual love and support. This is the magic of the real-life love relationships that women forge over and between consuming femme fictions.

In our current meantime, women may be commodities for exchange, but the upside is that we get to spend far more time in the closet. By this I mean not the closet where we're alone, or worse, getting fucked by Big, but the place where the other women are stored—the female space where we get to be ourselves with other women. As psychologists (e.g., Esther Perel) and historians of marriage (e.g., Stephanie Coontz) have noted, our present-day iteration of marriage is peculiar and fraught in that so much is resting on the sexual pair bond. Not only do we spend way too much time with our partners, but we expect them to be too much to us. They must satisfy us sexually, emotionally, spiritually, economically, and practically. We have to have great sex with the same person with whom we have to pay the bills and do the dishes and the laundry, not to mention raise the children and talk about our dreams and feelings and go on vacations and bring as our date to work events. It's an impossible set of requirements for any one person to meet—let alone a person who has been socialized in precisely the opposite way and for whom (if he is a man) the dictates of gender and how they affect women have been rendered invisible or at least impossible to fully comprehend. Heterosexuality may thoroughly suck in a heterosexist culture, but it's also an orientation shaped by that culture. I've come to recognize how, in order to live inside of that culture, we've intertwined our guilt and shame with our pleasure—the very forces that oppress us have also come to excite us.

If the consumption of guilty pleasure texts is a solution to finding spaces of joy within the vastness of the meantime, spaces where femme subjects can access a cathartic pleasure at the spectacle of domination, it seems to follow that the dream of a new system of cultural values, one that eliminates domination, would not include these texts. In *All About Love* (2000), bell hooks writes that love cannot be present in a system of domination, a truism I struggle to contend with because it implies that within our current reality, defined by structures of domination as it is, there can be no love. But, at the same time, hooks describes the communities of love she's been able to create and inhabit within that culture. She finally arrives at her own solution—to choose love in her practices of daily life, to overcome fear and the prospect of humiliation (which, in our current culture, attends the very wish for love). The theorist Gayle Rubin, who also writes about Mead's Arapesh yams, articulates her dream society as "androgynous and gender-less (though not sexless)." I see the merit in that, for sure. But I also think gender can be fun and feel good once it is dislodged from the mandate to, as Rubin also writes, "transform biological sexuality into products of human activity." The problem here seems to me to be neither gender nor biological sexuality but the need to create "products." Wedding films like *Romy and Michele's* and *Muriel's Wedding* dislodge that need by refusing to pair off their heroines. Once these women release themselves from the pressures of becoming a bride, they can enjoy being women.

I dream of a world wherein sexual dominance play is just play, wherein I can accept the gift of a ring or wear any dress I so choose without the fear of becoming property. I long to watch a film about people who have nice things and live relatively stress-free lives because they deserve them, as we all do. I used to think that femme fictions used plots of the longing for love to explore the wages of political domination. Now I know that political domination is itself a manifestation of the unanswered human wish for unconditional love and acceptance. If I were to consume all of the texts I've described herein while living in some postcapitalist, postheteropatriarchal utopia, I wonder if I'd find at the end that they were simply celebrations of the gratification of that wish.

CODA

I wrote this book in the summer of 2020, during the onset of a global pandemic and the seemingly sudden nationwide realization that we do, indeed, live in a country built on the legacy of human exploitation and murder. At the same time, I also found myself at the end of my marriage. In September 2019, I nearly died amid a series of bizarre and unexpected medical events occasioned by the patriarchal medical establishment's refusal to recognize female pain. Shortly after I recovered, three of my oldest friends decided to take me on a birthday trip to the Grand Canyon. I'd never been to the Grand Canyon before, and when I thought I might not live, I became weirdly fixated on this fact. (This is partly because a few years prior I stood in stupefied awe at the rim of the Grand Canyon of the Yellowstone and overheard a woman beside me say to her daughter, "Well, it's not nearly as impressive as the Grand Canyon.")

The four of us went to a spa and a very fancy dinner—like, with foam-food—to celebrate my birthday. The following day, we drove to the canyon, belting out femme pop songs in the car. When we arrived, we all hopped out at the same time and began profusely swearing, gobsmacked by the physical beauty all around us. (The woman at the Grand Canyon of the Yellowstone was, as it turns out, right.) We became convinced of the feminine power of the Earth in that spot, bought crystals and tarot cards, drank rosé and told stories in the hot tub. It was the most romantic weekend of my entire life.

As I find my way back to heterosexual love after my divorce, I'm using the romance of my female friendships as a map. Even though I have a notoriously bad sense of direction geographically speaking, this emotional map has been pretty easy for me to follow. My marriage was fraught from the very beginning, in the sense that it was forged under mandates (political, economic, biological) to exchange and produce. Divorce illuminates the property-based terms of marriage very starkly. One must list all of the marriage's holdings and products: the car, the house, the bank accounts, the children. The initial love that created the relationship is not accounted for in these lists. The very terms of divorce suggest that it has vanished in legal language that states, for example, "the parties knowingly and voluntarily shall and do hereby mutually release, remise and forever discharge each other from any and all claims, demands, and obligations whatsoever, both in law and in equity, which either of them ever had, now has, or may hereafter have, against the other upon or by reason of their marital relationship or any other matter, cause, or thing up to the date of this agreement."

Property can be equitably divided, but the mutual "claims, demands, and obligations" of love cannot. These, both by law and practice, simply evaporate upon the dissolution of love. Love can be neither stored nor hoarded. It cannot properly, I think, even be exchanged.

When we love well within the context of heteropatriarchal capitalism, it might appear as though we are acting against our own best interests. Guilty pleasures celebrate this in the trope of being foolish for love (*Fool for Love* [1984], *Fools Rush In* [1997], *Crazy, Stupid, Love* [2011], etc.). But this foolishness is, in fact, a kind of wisdom. By acting strictly on a principle of self-preservation, we may survive, but we will never flourish. My heart aches for those who refuse to wear a mask to protect other people in their community from becoming sick because they fear losing their own abstract idea of freedom or those who are more concerned about the protection of their property than the lives of their neighbors. These desires communicate to me that those who experience them have given up on love, that they believe wholeheartedly that they will never be supported by others or accepted for themselves. They communicate a conviction that no one else will act outside of self-interest toward them because of love or respect for them. They are, in effect, the positions of the emotionally dispossessed.

I feel fortunate to have never felt this way, and I think I have femme fictions to thank for this. If my female friends provided my current map of love, my books provided my first. As a child among my shelves, I felt connected to the voices from the past calling out to me from their pages in sisterhood. They were writing to me, I thought, without the demand that I respond or give anything back.

Much of what I've done in my professional life so far has been an effort to repay the debts I have incurred along the way, not only to the teachers and mentors who have guided me but also to the writers who have shaped my consciousness. Like many educators, I'm often gifted words of gratitude by my students. But what I understand myself to be doing is not for their benefit. It's for the benefit of the writers and teachers who have educated me. This kind of gift can never be an exchange. If the woman is the commodity whose exchange solidifies relations between patriarchal kinship groups, a text can be a noncommodity shared by generations of readers, binding them through a gift of feelings and ideas that asks for nothing in return.

When we are in love, everything the beloved does is precious and endearing. We're enthralled by the beauty of their mere presence, by the way they put things into words and the faces they make when they speak them. To approach our cultural texts with love is, I think, a step toward approaching the world with love. As a critic, I have been trained to mine texts for their flaws and contradictions. This taught me, also, to mine the world for its problems. One needn't dig very deeply to be rewarded there. But what does the world look like from a place of enthrallment? What solutions emerge when we momentarily cease trying to produce outcomes or answers but instead engage in celebration? Recent shows like *Schitt's Creek* seek to address social problems like homophobia by celebrating same-sex love rather than arguing against or even depicting the heterosexist logic that hates it. Maybe that's a start.

If the experience of writing this book has taught me anything, it's that there are many different kinds of love and they needn't even be "real" or "true" to work. In *The State of Affairs*, Esther Perel writes that she "meet[s] consumers of the modern ideology of marriage" in her office every day. "They take their relational aspirations as a given—both what they want and what they deserve to have—and are upset when the romantic ideal doesn't jibe with the unromantic reality." Many people asked me, as I researched and worked on this project, what impact so much rewatching and rereading of "romantic fairy tales" was having on my psyche. They asked if I thought that consuming these idealistic and even damaging fictions would make me unsatisfied with love or my lot in life as a heterosexual woman. If anything, I now think that a real-life commitment to finding "true" love—and especially true romantic love—as a static state is a more profound delusion than the delirious visions offered by femme fictions. Embracing the fictional fantasy of love only underscores that. Such fictions allow us to identify and enjoy the fantastic in life as such, however it may come.

Love may always be a little wrongheaded, dangerous, and idealistic. Carrie Bradshaw is right, in the end, when she differentiates between logic and love. Love must contain a risk, a vulnerable undoing and exposure of our most humiliating selves. It may always, therefore, be something we must approach as blindfolded, insecure, and naïve. I think that's brave. Love is the ultimate pleasure without product. To turn away from the parts of our culture that may occasionally make us wince is to reject the body we collectively inhabit for its vulnerabilities. I choose, instead, to love the body and the brace of it all, without fear or judgment. Stevie Wonder sings in "As," which perhaps makes every single point I advance in these pages much better than I do, "Make sure when you say you're in it but not of it, you're not helping to make this earth a place sometimes called hell. Change your words into truths and then change that truth into love, and maybe our children's grandchildren and their great-great-grandchildren will tell I'll be loving you." Love will not change our political structures. We must make love itself the structure. And, in the meantime, dear reader, I'll be loving you, too—please pass it on.

Acknowledgments

Thank you to Eric Zinner, Dolma Ombadykow, Laura Ewan, Martin Coleman, Andrew Katz, and Furqan Sayeed at NYU Press. Series editors Sarah Mesle and Sarah Blackwood: I am so grateful for your brilliance, time, insight, and support throughout this project and others. Our friendship teaches me much and remains a pure pleasure. I am also indebted to my research assistants, Alyssa Canepa and Alex Rickert, for chasing speculations and confirming when shit is bananas.

This book would not be possible without the people I've had the benefit of thinking with over the years: Laura Korobkin, who first introduced me to sentimental fiction; Linda Marrow, who first introduced me to the very serious business of romance novels; Jim Longenbach, who long urged me to write "the kind of book that doesn't have citations"; John Levi Barnard and Justine Murison, dear friends who encouraged me to prioritize this project above all else; my graduate adviser, Susan Mizruchi; Julia Brown; Erin Murphy; Charlotte Herscher; Dana Isaacson; Beth Wareham; Heather Holcombe; Emily Field; Iain Bernhoft; Jonathan Deschere; Christian

Engley; Heather Barrett; Claire Kervin; Maggie Vinter; Julia Whyde; Sarah Colvert; Cara Rodriguez; Jackie Bradley; Brianna Casey; Danielle Pafunda; Erin Forbes; Shari Goldberg; Donna Campbell; Jack Halberstam; Cynthia Davis; Autumn Womack; Laura Fisher; Tara MacDonald; Melissa Gniadek; Faye Halpern; Emily Orlando; Margaret Jay Jesse; Meg Toth; Myrto Drizou; Sarah Allison; Ayelet Ben-Yishai; Kristin Allukian; Hunt Howell; Marie McDonough; David Singerman; Jennifer Roberts; Joanna Scott; Alexander Southgate; Michael Colin; Shaun Galanos; Anya Kamenetz; Matthew Stratton; Lilia Soto; Barbara Logan; Tara Clapp; Allison Gernant; Peter Parolin; Caroline McCracken-Flesher; Susan Aronstein; Nina McConigley; Mike and Evelyn Edson; Mimi Fenton; Nancy Small; and Kelly Kinney, a superb department chair and friend who provided both material and intellectual support for this work.

I'm grateful to the Society for the Study of American Women Writers, an organization that has long nurtured the scholarship of female-authored texts and the careers of female scholars.

Thank you to my family: the Zibraks, especially my parents, who encouraged my love of books, created space for my choices, and bought a lot of dance costumes, and Bari, who is most certainly a feminist; the Sollods; the Rifkins; and the Pedersons, especially Jonah, who always asks the best questions about love.

My deepest thanks go to the women who have become my chosen family. Mary Kuhn—may we always be each other's Nancies. Julia Obert—you have taught me so much about intimacy both on and off the page. Brandi Shah—from our first poetry seminar together, you have continually inspired me with your wisdom and capacity for big, deep feelings. Elise Metzger, who has danced with me from the very beginning of our lives—I couldn't have gotten through all of the things, let alone written this book, without you in my heart and on the other end of so many texts and phone calls. Marissa Gemma can always be counted on to tell hard truths with unconditional love and was quarantined with me while I wrote the better part of this book; MG—"when we both get older / with walking canes and hair of gray / have no fear even though it's hard to hear / I will stand here close and say / thank you for being a friend."

Bibliography

Ahmed, Sarah. *Living a Feminist Life.* Durham, NC: Duke University Press, 2017.

Als, Hilton. *White Girls.* San Francisco: McSweeney's, 2013.

Baldwin, James. *Notes of a Native Son.* Boston: Beacon, 1955.

Beauvoir, Simone de. *The Second Sex.* 1949. Translated by H. M. Parshley. London: Penguin, 1972.

Benjamin, Jessica. *The Bonds of Love: Psychoanalysis, Feminism and the Problem of Domination.* New York: Pantheon, 1988.

Berlant, Lauren. *The Female Complaint: The Unfinished Business of Sentimentality in American Culture.* Durham, NC: Duke University Press, 2008.

Brown, Brené. *Daring Greatly: How the Courage to Be Vulnerable Transforms the Way We Live, Love, Parent, and Lead.* New York: Avery, 2012.

Chu, Andrea Long. *Females.* London: Verso, 2019.

Coontz, Stephanie. *Marriage, a History: How Love Conquered Marriage.* New York: Penguin, 2006.

Fisher, Mark. *Capitalist Realism.* Winchester, UK: Zero Books, 2009.

Foucault, Michel. *The History of Sexuality, Volume 1: An Introduction.* 1976. Translated by Robert Hurley. New York: Vintage Books, 1990.

Freeman, Elizabeth. *The Wedding Complex: Forms of Belonging in Modern American Culture.* Durham, NC: Duke University Press, 2002.

Gay, Roxane. *Bad Feminist*. New York: Harper, 2014.

———. *Hunger*. New York: Harper, 2017.

Girard, René. *Deceit, Desire, and the Novel: Self and Other in Literary Structure*. Baltimore: Johns Hopkins University Press, 1976.

Harris-Perry, Melissa. *Sister Citizen: Shame, Stereotypes, and Black Women in America*. New Haven, CT: Yale University Press, 2011.

Hartman, Saidiya. "The End of White Supremacy, An American Romance." *Bomb Magazine*, June 5, 2020. https://bombmagazine.org.

———. *Wayward Lives, Beautiful Experiments: Intimate Histories of Riotous Black Girls, Troublesome Women, and Queer Radicals*. London: Profile, 2019.

hooks, bell. *All About Love: New Visions*. New York: Harper, 2000.

Hopper, Briallen. *Hard to Love*. London: Bloomsbury, 2019.

Houppert, Karen. *The Curse: Confronting the Last Unmentionable Taboo: Menstruation*. New York: Macmillan, 2000.

Jameson, Fredric. *The Political Unconscious: Narrative as a Socially Symbolic Act*. Ithaca, NY: Cornell University Press, 1981.

Jarvis, Claire. *Exquisite Masochism: Marriage, Sex, and the Novel Form*. Baltimore: Johns Hopkins University Press, 2016.

Kendall, Mikki. *Hood Feminism: Notes from the Women That a Movement Forgot*. New York: Viking, 2020.

Krentz, Jane Anne. Introduction to *Dangerous Men and Adventurous Women: Romance Writers on the Appeal of the Romance*, edited by Jane Anne Krentz. Philadelphia: University of Pennsylvania Press, 1992.

Lorde, Audre. *The Master's Tools Will Never Dismantle the Master's House*. New York: Penguin, 2018.

Mead, Margaret. *From the South Seas: Studies of Adolescence and Sex in Primitive Societies*. New York: Morrow, 1939.

Merish, Lori. *Sentimental Materialism: Gender, Commodity Culture, and Nineteenth-Century American Literature*. Durham, NC: Duke University Press, 2000.

Mesle, Sarah. "A Television of Her Own: On Emily Nussbaum." *LARB: Los Angeles Review of Books*, August 30, 2019. https://lareviewofbooks.org.

Moore, Carly. "The Invasion of the Everygirl: *Seventeen* Magazine, 'Traumarama!' and the Girl Writer." *Journal of Popular Culture* 44, no. 6 (2011): 1248–67.

Moorhead, Liz. "Devil in a White Dress." *Washington Post*, September 14, 2018. www.washingtonpost.com.

Morrison, Toni. *Playing in the Dark: Whiteness and the Literary Imagination*. Cambridge, MA: Harvard University Press, 1992.

Noble, Marianne. *The Masochistic Pleasures of Sentimental Literature*. Princeton, NJ: Princeton University Press, 2000.

Perel, Esther. *Mating in Captivity: Unlocking Erotic Intelligence*. New York: Harper, 2018.

———. *The State of Affairs: Rethinking Infidelity*. New York: Harper, 2017.

Phillips, Adam. "The Simplicity of Shame." *Salmagundi*, Spring–Summer 2019.

Plott, Michelle, and Lauri Umansky. *Making Sense of Women's Lives: An Introduction to Women's Studies*. Lanham, MD: Rowman and Littlefield, 2000.

Radway, Janice. *Reading the Romance: Women, Patriarchy and Popular Literature*. 1984. Rev. ed. Chapel Hill: University of North Carolina Press, 1990.

Regis, Pamela. *A Natural History of the Romance Novel*. Philadelphia: University of Pennsylvania Press, 2013.

Roberson, Blythe. *How to Date Men When You Hate Men*.
New York: Flatiron Books, 2018.

Rubin, Gayle. "The Traffic in Women: Notes on the 'Political
Economy' of Sex." In *Toward an Anthropology of Women*,
edited by Rayna R. Reiter, 157–210. New York: Monthly
Review Press, 1975.

Sedgwick, Eve Kosofsky. *The Epistemology of the Closet*.
Berkeley: University of California Press, 1990.

Sow, Aminatou, and Ann Friedman. *Big Friendship: How We
Keep Each Other Close*. New York: Simon and Schuster,
2020.

Tan, Candy, and Sarah Wendell. *Beyond Heaving Bosoms:
The Smart Bitches' Guide to Romance Novels*. New York:
Simon and Schuster, 2009.

Taylor, Helen. *Why Women Read Fiction: The Stories of Our
Lives*. Oxford: Oxford University Press, 2020.

Trilling, Lionel. *The Liberal Imagination*. New York: Viking,
1950.

Wardrop, Daneen. *Emily Dickinson and the Labor of Clothing*. Lebanon: University of New Hampshire Press, 2009.

Welter, Barbara. "The Cult of True Womanhood: 1820–1860."
American Quarterly 18, no. 2 (1966): 151–74.

About the Author

Arielle Zibrak is Associate Professor of English and Gender and Women's Studies at the University of Wyoming.